ROUGH CUT
WOODWORKING WITH TOMMY MAC

ROUGH CUT
WOODWORKING WITH TOMMY MAC

12 STEP-BY-STEP PROJECTS

Tommy MacDonald
with Laurie Donnelly

The Taunton Press

The Taunton Press
Inspiration for hands-on living®

THE TAUNTON PRESS, INC.,
63 South Main Street, PO Box 5506, Newtown, CT 06470-5506
e-mail: tp@taunton.com

Editor: **SCOTT GIBSON**
Copy Editor: **CANDACE B. LEVY**
Indexer: **CATHY GODDARD**
Cover design: **JEAN-MARC TROADEC, DESIGN & TYPOGRAPHY**
Interior design: **NICK CARUSO**
Layout: **CATHY CASSIDY**
Illustrator: **BOB LA POINTE**
Cover photography: **ANTHONY TIEULI**
Photographers: **ANTHONY TIEULI FOR PBS DISTRIBUTION (FRONT COVER; BACK COVER, RIGHT; P. 18);
THOMAS MOORE (PP. 4, 32, 44, 58, 70, 82, 96, 106, 120, 140, 154, 162)**

The following names/manufacturers appearing in *Rough Cut—Woodworking with Tommy Mac*
are trademarks: Styrofoam®

Library of Congress Cataloging-in-Publication Data

MacDonald, Tommy.

 Rough cut : woodworking with Tommy Mac : 12 step-by-step projects / Tommy MacDonald with Laura Donnelly.

  p. cm.

 Includes index.

 ISBN 978-1-60085-416-3

 1. Furniture Making--Amateurs' manuals. 2. Woodwork--Amateurs' manuals. I. Donnelly, Laura. II. Title.

 TT195.M3185 2011

 684'.08--dc23

                        2011029445

Printed in the United States of America
10 9 8 7 6 5 4 3 2 1

For *Rough Cut—Woodworking with Tommy Mac*
television show

Host: **THOMAS J. MACDONALD**
Executive Producer & Director: **LAURIE DONNELLY**
Special guests: **STEVE BROWN, ELI CLEVELAND, AL D'ATTANASIO**
Producers: **THOMAS J. MACDONALD, LAURIE DONNELLY,
DAVID MASHER, ANNE ADAMS**
Coordinating Producer: **DEBORAH J. HURLEY**
Editorial Consultant: **STEVE BROWN, CABINET AND FURNITURE
MAKING DEPARTMENT, NORTH BENNET STREET SCHOOL**
Director of Photography: **STEPHEN D'ONOFRIO**
Audio: **MARK AREES**
Online Editor: **DAVE ALLEN**
Production Assistants: **ELI CLEVELAND, TOM GOTT**
Music: **DAVID MASHER & CRIT HARMON**
Graphics: **DAVID MASHER & INVERSION MEDIA**
Make-up: **SONJA GJOKAJ, ELIZABETH MOON**
National marketing: **PETER PANAGOPOULOS, TARA RAFIEYMEHR**
Station relations: **NANCY BOCCHINO, VICTORIA YUEN**
Special thanks: **THE NORTH BENNET STREET SCHOOL**
© **WGBH EDUCATIONAL FOUNDATION 2010**

ABOUT YOUR SAFETY

Working wood is inherently dangerous. Using hand or power tools improperly or ignoring safety practices can lead to permanent injury or even death. Don't try to perform operations you learn about here (or elsewhere) unless you're certain they are safe for you. If something about an operation doesn't feel right, don't do it. Look for another way. We want you to enjoy the craft, so please keep safety foremost in your mind whenever you're in the shop.

Dedication from Tommy
To the first person who put a hammer in my hand—my hero,
my father, James A. MacDonald. Thanks, Pops, for everything.

ACKNOWLEDGMENTS

From Tommy

I would like to thank WGBH and public television for pioneering how-to television, especially in the field of home improvement and woodworking. Their programming inspired me, at an early age, to pick up a hammer for the very first time.

Our series, *Rough Cut—Woodworking with Tommy Mac*, would never have happened without the vision, guidance, and help of executive producer and co-writer Laurie Donnelly, who has gone to bat for me since day one. Laurie along with Margaret Drain, David Bernstein, Peter McGee, Anne Adams, Tara Rafieymehr, Nancy Bocchino, Victoria Yuen, and the rest of the WGBH team have worked tirelessly to make my vision a reality.

I would also like to give a heartfelt thanks to Sam Ross, Jeff Forbes, and Jody Garrett, without whose support this series would not have been possible. They, along with Dawn Knowst, Liz Byers, Laurie Milner, all of the product guys and the wonderful network of independent Woodcraft franchise owners, have made me feel proud to be a part of the Woodcraft family. Together we all share a commitment to keep a seasoned generation of woodworkers inspired while igniting interest among a new generation just coming into the fold.

I also want to give a shout out to my Rough Cut television team—David Masher, Eli Cleveland, Al D'Attanasio, Steve Brown, Steve D'Onofrio, Mark Libby, Tom Jackson, and David Cohen—who have been deep in the production trenches right along with me.

There would also be no *Rough Cut— Woodworking with Tommy Mac* without the shop teachers who taught and guided me. From my early days at the Galvin Middle School to high school at the Blue Hills Voc Tech, then continuing on through my union carpentry apprentice program and finishing up with the Cabinet Furniture Program at Boston's North Bennet Street School— each stop along the way not only has helped me to perfect my craft but also has taught me some great life lessons.

And in the spirit of it takes a village to raise a woodworker, I extend a special thanks to all my friends (you know who you are) along with Jock Gifford, who always believed in me; the staff at Elite Health and Fitness Center, especially Peter Rappoli, who keeps me mentally focused and physically fit, and Robert Ayer, who is always willing to lend a helping hand.

A big thanks to my entire family for their love and support, including my brother James and his family and my sister Susan and her husband, John, (along with their two kids Rebecca and Tommy), all of whom have helped keep me going.

I also want to thank my wife, Rachel, for her unwavering faith, support, and love that she has given me since the first day we met. There is no question that she makes me a better person.

Finally, I want to thank the community of woodworkers who enjoy woodworking just as much as I do. It's truly a labor of love.

From Laurie

My love and thanks to my family—Bill, Kate, and Lydia—for the support they show day in and day out.

CONTENTS

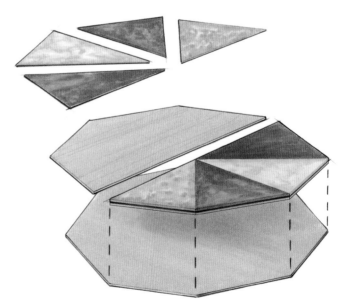

INTRODUCTION

The whole idea behind *Rough Cut—Woodworking with Tommy Mac* was for the show to be a catalyst for getting people acquainted with, or reacquainted with, something I love and feel passionate about—woodworking. Whether you have a big shop or small, whether it's tucked in the corner of the garage or down in the basement, you can work with wood in a way that brings joy to your life.

Although most of us are faced with the challenge of finding time for ourselves, woodworking is a gift of time you can give yourself to create something beautiful and memorable, even if you can find only a half-hour a day or a few hours a month.

In creating this Public Television series, we also felt passionately about the need to relieve people of the burden of feeling like they need to get everything "just right" and do things perfectly. It's OK to make mistakes; it's OK to get frustrated. We want people who watch our show and read this book to take home a simple message—give yourself a break.

When you get right down to it, woodworking is simple. I am not saying that it's easy—it does require time, patience, perseverance, and the willingness to flow with the learning process. It also demands that you allow yourself to work outside your comfort zone and feel challenged. When you do, it's amazing how much you'll also learn about yourself in the process. And that's where the fun of woodworking really lives.

The other thing that I love about woodworking is that when you make a mistake, it's abundantly clear what went wrong. On the upside, it's only wood, and there's more where that came from. If you're like me, you'll probably fill your scrap bins a mile high with all of those teachable moments!

With woodworking, just like anything else you want to learn in life, you need to allow yourself time on the learning curve. What you want to avoid is having your frustrations bring you to a standstill because you're feeling so overwhelmed and stifled by the need for perfection. Like I said before, it's not easy. I have found over the years that the ability to learn woodworking is not unlike riding a bike—it's inevitable that you'll endure a few bumps and bruises along on the way.

What I firmly believe is that this hobby is intended for everyone, not just the chosen few who happen to have a few bucks. People can build the projects found in the pages of this book using just a simple set of hand tools and power tools. And when it comes to materials, you'll be surprised at the remarkable results you can achieve from inexpensive woods—though you'll probably want to treat yourself to an occasional piece of something exotic.

Keep in mind that sometimes it's also nice to join forces with others—it makes the work even more enjoyable. I learned that firsthand at North Bennet Street School, where I was taught my trade. I enjoyed the camaraderie of working alongside people of all ages and backgrounds, and it was great to see how people approached woodworking in their own unique (and sometimes quirky) way. Today, on any given day, people are always dropping by my workshop in Canton, Massachusetts, sharing their ideas, hanging out, banging a few nails around. I get a kick out of it—at least on most days! *Rough Cut—Woodworking with Tommy Mac* embodies that same spirit of working with a community of people and having fun with woodworking.

The road trips we took during our first season of the show also confirmed that the passion for woodworking is not only alive and well but very much on the rise. We visited some of the country's top museums and master woodworkers as well as some hidden workshops. As you'll see on the show and in this book, there's inspiration to be found everywhere and something to be learned from every fellow woodworker.

It's time to get cracking. In this book you'll find the first 12 projects presented in our show, plus a chapter on finishing. We want you to be part of our *Rough Cut*

community by digging in and trying one or all of these projects. And if you don't want to create these projects just as they are, feel free to alter them in a way that makes them uniquely your own. Each one is based on a technique you'll want to learn whether you're new to woodworking or have been around the bench awhile. Together the projects represent a broad range of skills you'll want to master; once you've gotten the hang of these skills, we hope you'll have the confidence to build anything.

SHAKER STEP STOOL

Hand-Cutting Through-Dovetails

This simple and utilitarian project doesn't require a lot of lumber, a lot of time, or a long list of tools. Its traditional Shaker design gives it a quiet beauty that's a good fit for any home.

The stool's small size and light weight make it easy to move around the house. It's helpful for reaching high shelves or cabinets in the kitchen, it offers a boost for small children who can't quite reach the sink, and it can be a perfect springboard for pets eager to join you on the bed.

For a beginning woodworker, this project is an excellent introduction to preparing stock and cutting dovetails by hand. Dovetailing is a fundamental joinery skill that may look intimidating to woodworkers who are just starting out. There are many ways to cut this strong, interlocking joint, including the unusual approach adopted by furniture master Allan Breed (learn more about my visit with Allan in the Road Trip sidebar on p. 12). My approach is more traditional and easy to learn.

This two-step stool is made from nine simple parts that require less than 12 bd. ft. of lumber. The parts include a tall and short side on each end, the steps, and three stretchers that provide additional bracing. A taper cut on the back of the side pieces helps make the stool less likely to tip backward when standing on the top step.

The height of the steps as well as the width of the step stool can be adjusted to suit individual needs. Material choice is just as personal. Almost any kind of wood will do.

Shaker Step Stool

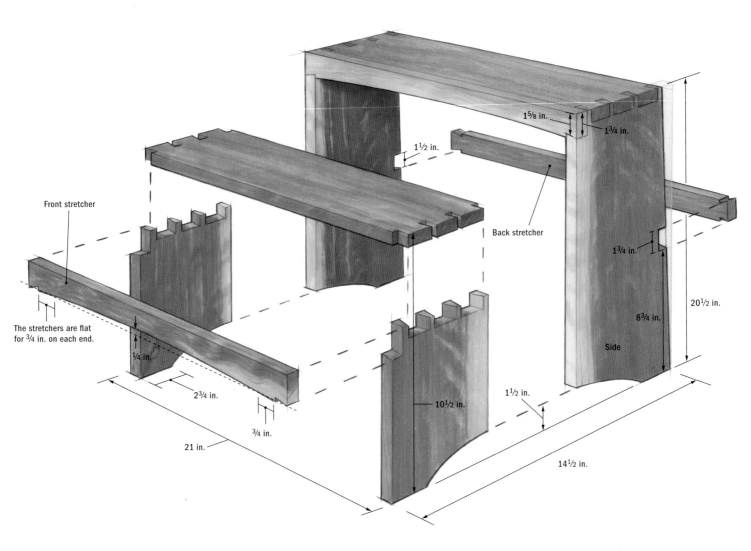

Front stretcher

The stretchers are flat for ¾ in. on each end.

¼ in.

2¾ in.

¾ in.

21 in.

1½ in.

Back stretcher

1⅝ in.

1¾ in.

1¾ in.

20½ in.

8¾ in.

Side

10½ in.

1½ in.

14½ in.

MATERIALS LIST/ROUGH MILL

PART	# OF PIECES	LENGTH (IN.)	WIDTH (IN.)	THICKNESS (IN.)	WOOD
Short side	2	11½	7¼	⅞	Primary
Tall side	2	21½	8¼	⅞	Primary
Step	2	22	6½	⅞	Primary
Stretcher	3	22	2¼	⅞	Primary

Rough dimensions are slightly longer, wider, and thicker than the finished dimensions. Mill the stock, sticker it overnight, and then bring pieces to the finished dimensions the following day.

Preparing stock

The butternut I'm using to build this step stool is 10 in. wide, 1 in. thick, and 11 ft. long in its rough form. Lay out all of the pieces for the stool working from a single plank; it's good practice to cut off a few inches from the end of the board (eliminating any checks and debris) to ensure a nice clean, solid, square end to start measuring from (**photo 1**).

Lay out the pieces. Pieces are marked out in chalk, slightly longer and slightly wider than their finished dimensions. This plank is wide enough for both a side piece and a stretcher, reducing waste to about nothing (**photo 2**). Labeling the pieces with chalk will prevent any mixups (**photo 3**).

TOOL LIST

POWER TOOLS
Bandsaw
Circular saw
Jigsaw
Jointer
Miter saw
Planer
Tablesaw

HAND TOOLS
Adjustable bevel
Chisels
Clamps
Combination
  square
Deadblow hammer
Dovetail saw
File
Handplane
Handsaw
Mallet
Marking gauge

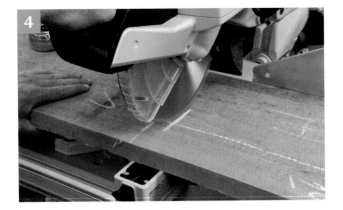

Safety First

When ripping material
on the tablesaw,
always use a splitter
and push stick
when the material
is narrower than a
hand's width.

Cut pieces to length. You can cut the pieces roughly to length with a handsaw, circular saw, or jigsaw. For this project a power miter saw connected to a dust collector served as a fast and accurate way to get the job done and keep the shop clean (**photo 4**). Separating the side pieces from the stretchers can be done on a bandsaw (**photo 5**).

Rough mill the stock. To rough mill the pieces, start with the jointer, flattening one face and jointing one edge, and then flatten the other face of each piece with a thickness planer. Remember to be aware of the grain direction when milling the wood to avoid tearout (see p. 23 for more on tearout).

Sticker the pieces overnight. After cutting the pieces to rough dimensions (about $3/16$ in. thicker, 1 in. longer, and $1/2$ in. wider than the finished dimensions), sticker them overnight. The next day remill the parts to their finished thickness, length, and width.

T-Mac Tip

Don't try to take too much material off in a single pass with the jointer or planer: $1/32$ in. to $1/16$ in. at a time is plenty. It's best to make a lighter cut in wood with gnarly grain.

Preparing the pieces for dovetails

Cutting through-dovetails is a two-step process. First, the pins are formed by cutting into the end of one piece and removing waste with a chisel and mallet. Then the corresponding tails are marked directly from the pins and cut out in the same way.

There are two dovetailed pieces for each side. After the dovetails are all cut, the pieces are edge-glued together to form a stepped side piece.

Set a marking gauge. Adjust a marking gauge to the thickness of the material (**photo 1**). This setting will be used to mark all of the pieces.

Mark the stretcher reference lines. There are three stretchers in the stool, one beneath the front edge of each step and one in the back. Mark the vertical cuts for the front stretchers in the side pieces with a marking gauge (**photo 2**), and then make the cuts on a tablesaw (**photo 3**) or with a handsaw. The depth of the cut should be less than the width of the stretcher.

Mark the baselines. With the marking gauge, work your way around the ends of all four side pieces and both ends of each step. These are the baselines where sawkerfs for the pins and tails will stop (**photo 4**).

Cut the taper. Before laying out and cutting the pins, taper the back edge. To do this, mark and cut the taper measuring in 1 in. from the top back edge to the bottom corner of the back edge. Cut

along the lines on both tall sides (**photo 5**). The tapers can be cut with a handsaw, bandsaw, or jigsaw (**photo 6**). Always clean up the cuts with a handplane.

T-Mac Tip

Save the offcut from cutting the tapers. It will be invaluable when gluing up the side pieces.

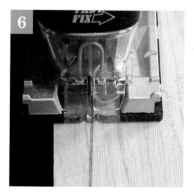

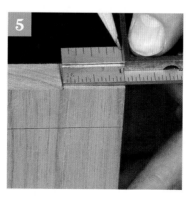

Understanding a Bench Plane

A bench plane is my tool of choice for removing mill marks left by a jointer and planer. While bench planes come in a variety of sizes, styles, and prices, they all have a lot of similarities **(photo 1).**

At the front of the plane is a knob and at the back a handle **(photo 2).** A locking lever **(photo 3)** clamps the two-part assembly of chip breaker and plane iron against an adjustable bed called a frog **(photo 4).** The frog can be moved forward or backward to change the opening in the throat of the plane—wider for heavy cuts, narrower for fine cuts in highly figured wood.

The key to good performance is a very sharp blade. No plane will do a good job if the blade is nicked or dull. I use a hollow grind on the edge of my plane blades **(photo 5).** First, the blade is dressed on a grinder, which leaves a slightly concave, or hollowed, surface. When the blade is honed on a sharpening stone, only two narrow bands of the blade actually

touch the stone. That makes it easier to keep the blade sharp between grindings because you need to remove only a small amount of material to restore the edge.

Once you put the sharp iron back in the plane, there are two adjustments to make: the depth of cut and the angle of the blade. Both will need to be finessed at the same time until you get a thin, constant shaving coming through the center of the throat **(photo 6)**.

Visiting a Dovetail Master

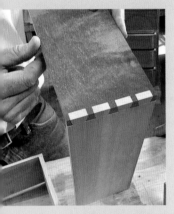
Through-dovetails

Dovetail joint

Half-blind dovetails

Allan Breed's work in classic American furniture forms is well known in the woodworking community, and I wanted to see how some of the period work, including dovetailing, is done at the Breed School of Fine Woodworking.

Dovetails are a key structural feature in many of the pieces Allan makes. The interlocking pins and tails of the dovetail joint make a very strong mechanical connection for casework as well as for drawers.

There are several types of dovetails: through-dovetails, which are visible from both sides of the joint (center photo at left), half-blind dovetails, seen from only one side (bottom photo at left), and the much more elaborate full-blind or mitered dovetail, which is hidden when the joint is assembled (photo below).

Allan's goal is to cut well-fitting dovetails quickly. He uses his tools, rather than a ruler or tape, to lay out the joints as much as possible and cuts the pins by eye. Perhaps his most unorthodox technique is cutting the tails with the saw held upside down, which he says helps make a plumb cut. The results speak for themselves.

Full-blind, or mitered, dovetails

Forming the pins

The pins are laid out on the ends of the side pieces. They are cut at a 1:6 angle, with the wider side of the pin facing the inside.

T-Mac Tip

Laying out the pins is a lot simpler if you have an L-shaped gauge block with the correct angle cut into both ends. I made mine from a piece of 1¾-in.-square stock. It can be used to make the angled layout line on the edge of the board as well as the square line down the face of the board.

Lay out the two end pins. The pins on each end are angled on only the inside. The outside edge is square to the face of the board. Mark a point ³⁄₈ in. from the edge and use the angled gauge block to mark the location of the end pins. (**photo 1**).

Mark the pin centerlines. Use a divider to mark the center points of each pin across the end of the board. It will take a little trial and error to get pins of the same width, and the spacing doesn't have to be perfect (**photo 2**).

Mark the pin widths. The width of the pins isn't critical. For this project I made them about ³⁄₄ in. wide at their widest point. Using the centerlines you just made, measure an equal distance out in each direction and mark the shoulders of each pin (**photo 3**). Now mark both edges of the pins using the wood gauge block or an adjustable bevel (**photo 4**).

Saw the pins. Using your thumb as a reference, line up the blade of the saw with the inside of the layout line and cut vertically to the baseline **(photo 5)**. Don't cut past the baseline.

Remove the waste. With the vertical cuts made, it's time to remove the waste between the pins. There are lots of ways to do this, including roughing out most of the work on a bandsaw. If you use a bandsaw, be sure to keep the wider part of the pin flat on the table so you don't cut the angled edge of the pin away. Make the straight cuts first, just inside the sawkerfs you've already made at the bench, then cut away the rest, making sure to stay inside the baseline **(photo 6)**.

Clean up the pins. After the piece comes off the bandsaw it will still have rough edges **(photo 7)**. Put a piece of plywood or other scrap material on your bench to protect it, then clamp the workpiece securely in place **(photo 8)**. With a very sharp chisel, work up to the baseline. When you get close, place the edge of the chisel right in the line left by the marking gauge and cut about halfway through the workpiece. Undercut the edge slightly so the pieces will fit together tightly **(photo 9)**. Flip the board over and finish removing the waste.

Glue up the sides. Once all the pins have been cleaned up, glue the two pairs of side pieces together. Use the tapered offcuts you set aside earlier between the clamps and the side pieces to keep the clamps square to the work.

Making the tails

The beauty of making dovetails by hand is that you mark out the tail pieces with the pins you've already cut. There's no measuring involved. As long as you cut to the layout lines accurately, the pieces will fit together nicely.

Mark the tail locations. Place a step face down on the bench and position the corresponding end piece directly on the layout line (**photo 1**). You can hold the end piece in place with a clamp. Make sure the edges of the two pieces are lined up, then mark along the edges of the pins with a pencil (**photo 2**).

Mark the end of the board. Using the ends of the tail layout lines as a reference, use a combination square to continue drawing the lines across the edge of the board (**photo 3**).

Cut to the baseline. Using the pencil lines as a reference, cut down to the baseline. Make absolutely sure to leave the whole thickness of the pencil line; otherwise the pieces will have a sloppy fit. It's better to have to pare the tails slightly than to have a loose fit (**photo 4**).

T-Mac Tip

To avoid going past the baseline on the top of the step, tip the saw back at a slight angle and creep up to the line carefully.

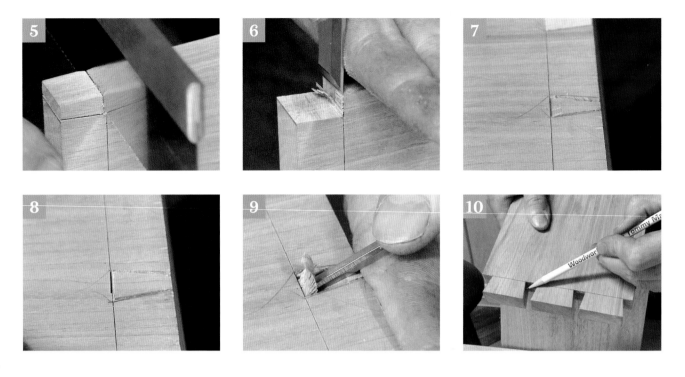

Cut away the side pieces.

Working on one outside edge, form a small shoulder at the baseline with a chisel, then cut away the waste with a saw (**photo 5**). Now pare to the line with a chisel (**photo 6**). Repeat on the other outside edge.

Chop out the middle.

To remove the waste in between the pins, start by creating a small shoulder at the baseline (**photo 7**) by pressing a chisel into the line, then taking out a small wedge-shape piece. When you use a mallet to chop out the waste, this shoulder will prevent the chisel from drifting over the line (**photo 8**).

With these shoulders created, you can tap a chisel into the line a little more aggressively. Use a smaller chisel to work toward the line and remove the waste as you go, but remember to leave some wood toward the outside edge for support (**photo 9**). Work about halfway through

the board, then flip it over. Repeat the process, this time removing all of the material between the tails.

Dry-fit the pieces.

After the pieces have been cleaned up and all material to the lines removed, it's time for a dry-fit. Put a side piece in the vise, and fit a corresponding step in place. Use your fist or a deadblow hammer to start fitting the two pieces together. If it feels too tight, remove the step and look for compressed wood, indicating where more material still needs to be removed (**photo 10**). Pare away those spots on the tail board until the two pieces fit together. Repeat the process on all four corners until the steps are snuggly attached to the sides.

T-Mac Tip

When tapping the steps into place with a deadblow hammer, use a board on edge across the width of the step so you don't mar the surface.

Final Steps

Make the front stretchers. Cut a 1:6 angle into the ends of the stretchers that go on the front of the stool. The dovetail is cut into the bottom edge only (**photo 1**). Then transfer the layout lines onto the front edges of the stool.

Make a back stretcher. Each end of the back stretcher is cut into a single dovetail, also at an angle of 1:6 (**photo 2**). After cutting the ends, lay the stretcher across the back and transfer the layout lines to the edges of the step.

Cut out the stretcher locations. With a handsaw and chisel, remove the waste where the stretchers go. When cutting along the layout lines, don't forget to leave the lines so you get an accurate fit (**photo 3**). Then clean up the joint with a chisel (**photo 4**).

Add some curves. To soften the look of the stool, cut a gentle radius into the bottom edges of the front stretchers using either a bandsaw or a jigsaw. Then make curved cutouts at the center of each side piece to help keep the stool from rocking (**photo 5**). Clean up the edges with a file and then sandpaper.

Glue-up and finish. After all of the pieces have been cleaned up, it's time for the final glue-up. For a finish, I use my favorite combination: a coat of linseed oil followed by super blonde shellac and, finally, wax. (For more on gluing up and finishing, see pp. 162–181.)

TRESTLE TABLE

Working with Mortise-and-Tenon Joinery

This classic trestle table is a good beginner's project because the construction is straightforward and easy to do. Based on a colonial American design, the table could be made from a slab of wood and two stands.

While more ornate detailing has been applied throughout the centuries, I decided to keep my piece simple. My design relies on wedged mortise-and-tenon joints that can be cut by machine or by hand, depending on what tools you have around the shop.

The base is made of two posts, four battens, and one stretcher. The top is glued up from several boards with spring joints to keep the boards tight. Personally, I am not a fan of biscuits, dowels, or splines because they don't add any real strength. While the breadboard ends are mostly decorative, they also help keep the top flat.

Keep in mind the design of a trestle table is flexible, so sizing it to fit your space is easy. This table measures 32 in. by 62 in., but it can be downsized or enlarged, depending on the size of your room. Changing the dimensions will not take away from the table's overall appeal.

Although the table could be built from just about any species of wood, this one is made from black walnut (see the Road Trip sidebar on p. 24 for more on hand-picking material). Walnut is durable and easy to work with and it has a deep, rich color, which is enhanced with the application of an oil and shellac finish.

Trestle Table

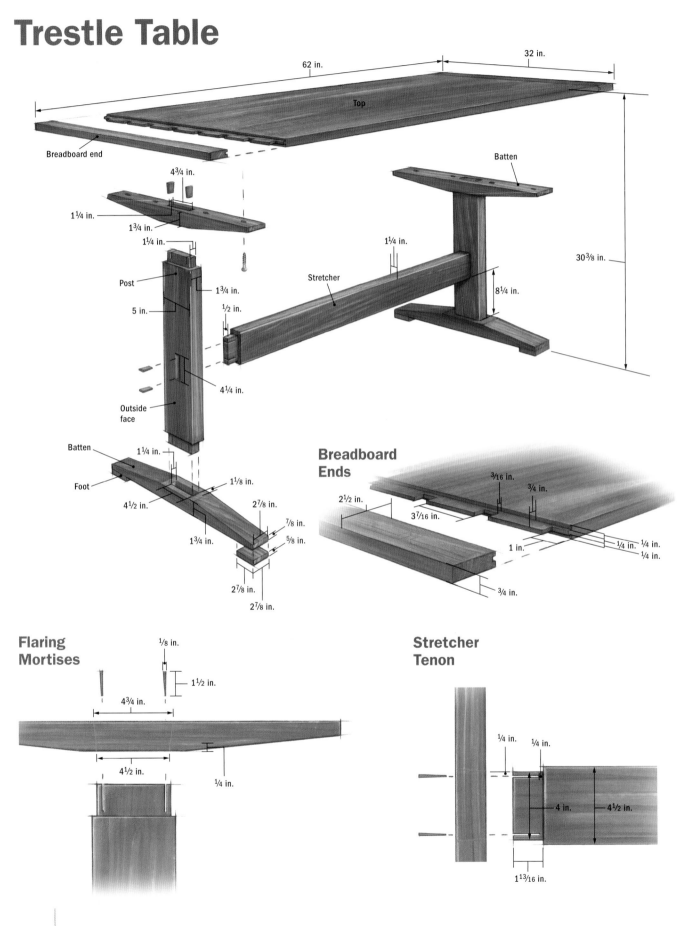

62 in.

32 in.

Top

Breadboard end

Batten

4³⁄₄ in.

1¹⁄₄ in.

1³⁄₄ in.

1¹⁄₄ in.

Post

1³⁄₄ in.

5 in.

¹⁄₂ in.

Stretcher

1¹⁄₄ in.

8¹⁄₄ in.

30³⁄₈ in.

4¹⁄₄ in.

Outside
face

Batten

1¹⁄₄ in.

Foot

4¹⁄₂ in.

1¹⁄₈ in.

2⁷⁄₈ in.

⁷⁄₈ in.

1³⁄₄ in.

⁵⁄₈ in.

2⁷⁄₈ in.

2⁷⁄₈ in.

Breadboard Ends

2¹⁄₂ in.

³⁄₁₆ in.

³⁄₄ in.

3⁷⁄₁₆ in.

1 in.

¹⁄₄ in.   ¹⁄₄ in.

¹⁄₄ in.

³⁄₄ in.

Flaring Mortises

¹⁄₈ in.

1¹⁄₂ in.

4³⁄₄ in.

4¹⁄₂ in.

¹⁄₄ in.

Stretcher Tenon

¹⁄₄ in.   ¹⁄₄ in.

4 in.

4¹⁄₂ in.

1¹³⁄₁₆ in.

MATERIALS LIST/ROUGH MILL

PART	# OF PIECES	LENGTH (IN.)	WIDTH (IN.)	THICKNESS (IN.)	WOOD	NOTES
Post	2	30	5½	1⅞	Primary	
Batten	4	27	3⅜	1⅞	Primary	
Stretcher	1	46½	5	1⅜	Primary	
Foot	4	3⅞	3⅜	¾	Primary	
Top	1	59½	32½	⅞	Primary	
Breadboard	2	33	3	⅞	Primary	
Screws	8					#8 × 1 in.

Rough dimensions are slightly larger, wider and thicker than the finished dimensions. Mill the stock, sticker it overnight, and then bring pieces to the finished dimensions the following day.

TOOLS

POWER TOOLS

Bandsaw
Circular saw
Cordless drill
Drill press
Jigsaw
Jointer
Mortising machine
Planer
Tablesaw with
    dado blade

HAND TOOLS

Chisels
Clamps
Combination
    square
Deadblow hammer
Dovetail saw
Handplanes
Mallet
Marking gauge
Marking knife

Rough milling the stock

Remove the waste. All the pieces for the base are made from one plank of walnut so there will be consistent color and a good grain match. The plank could have a few checks, dirt, pebbles, or staples on the ends so it's good to get into the habit of removing the first couple of inches before marking out any parts **(photo 1)**. Mark the cutline with chalk then make the cut with a circular saw **(photo 1)**. A thick plank like this one has to be cut from both sides.

Lay out the base pieces. The parts are laid out with chalk on the face of the board (see the Materials List above). These are just rough reference lines, not drawn to a finished dimension, so they should be an inch or so longer and about ½ in. wider than what the finished part will be. To avoid confusion, label each piece as you go **(photo 2)**.

Cut the pieces to rough size. Now the plank can be cut into rough parts (**photo 3**). I have a bandsaw in my shop for making the long cuts, but if you don't have one, just continue using a circular saw.

Clean the surface. Use a wire brush to clean the boards. Then take a good look at each surface and make sure there are no embedded stones or pieces of metal that could damage your tools.

Check the jointer. The next step is to flatten one face and then joint one edge. Check to make sure the fence and the bed of the jointer are at a perfect 90 degrees (**photo 4**). Remember, you can flatten the face and joint the edge with a handplane if you don't have a jointer.

Flatten one face. Before running the piece over the jointer you need to find the direction of the grain. For me, the easiest way of determining this is by rubbing the face of the board with my hand. When going with the grain it feels smooth. Take a piece of chalk and mark on the edge of the board an arrow that indicates the right direction. You're then ready to run the board over the

cutterhead (**photo 5**). If you go in the wrong direction on the jointer it will be abundantly clear from the tearout. Just flip the board end for end and continue until the face of the board is flat (**photo 6**).

   Plane to rough thickness. After flattening one face of each piece, move to the thickness planer. Set the dial so the planer is taking off $\frac{1}{16}$ in. of material and put the board through the planer with the arrow facing out and the flattened side down on the table (**photo 7**). Plane the pieces until they are slightly thicker, $\frac{1}{8}$ in. to $\frac{3}{16}$ in., more than the finished dimension, then clean up one edge on the jointer (**photo 8**).

   Cut to width. Cut the pieces roughly to width on the tablesaw. Make all of the pieces slightly bigger, $\frac{1}{2}$ in. or

so, than the finished dimension (see the drawings on p. 20).

T-Mac Tip

When setting the height of the tablesaw blade, bring the blade up so about half the gullet, the space between teeth, is above the stock.

   Sticker the pieces overnight. Once all of the pieces have been rough milled, it's a good idea to leave them stickered overnight to allow good air flow around them while they acclimate to their new shape and size (**photo 9**). The next day repeat the milling process on the jointer, planer, and tablesaw to bring all the pieces down to their final dimensions.

Hand-Picking Material

Old-growth tree ready for milling

Bandsaw mill

Board free of checking and cracking

Searching out a company that does custom sawing has several advantages, and topping the list is that you'll find a lumberyard full of wide, clear boards that are good enough to build world-class furniture. In a lot of cases, the wood comes from private yards, which means it is from old-growth trees and has the kind of quality that is generally less available in your average lumberyard.

Another advantage is that you can have the fun of picking through what's on hand and selecting boards with the best color and figure for your individual project.

Custom lumberyards use a bandsaw mill to cut the planks. Once the sapwood is sliced away, some really nice planks begin to emerge, as shown in the bottom photo at left.

After the tree has been cut into planks, the boards are stickered tree by tree and left to dry. This drying process takes about a year per inch of thickness. Boards are stacked in sequential order to ensure that woodworkers get consistent grains, tones, and textures, which is ideal when building a large piece of furniture or when making several pieces for the same room.

The lumber that has been set aside for this table is especially beautiful and will let me get a clear top that's free of knots. There's also plenty of length here to cut away the problem areas.

T-Mac Tip

Often the best board in the tree will be the third plank in. By then, the sapwood is mostly gone and the board is still far from the pith at the center of the tree, where checking and cracking are more common.

Stickered boards, stacked in sequential order

Black walnut board ready for the shop

Joinery: First, the mortises

Remove the mill marks. Before getting into the joinery, all of the mill marks left from the jointer and planer should be removed. I use a no. 4 or 4½ smoothing plane. The blade should be very sharp (**photo 1**). (See pp. 10–11 for more information on sharpening the blade.) Just as you did before jointing the lumber, rub your hand across the face of the board to find the direction of the grain (**photo 2**). Use your handplane so it cuts with the grain, and don't take too much material off in one pass. Remove just enough to eliminate the mill marks as you work your way across the board (**photo 3**).

Lay out the mortises. The table is assembled with mortise-and-tenon joints. The mortises in the battens and posts get cut first; I use a marking knife and a marking gauge to lay them out. Mark the dimensions of each mortise with a pencil first, then use the knife to mark the ends of the mortise and use the marking gauge to mark the edges (**photo 4**).

Cut the mortises. I use a mortising machine. If you don't have one you can cut the mortises with a drill press, a drill, and a chisel, or even a chisel and a mallet. Set up the machine so the mortising chisel is lined up with the layout mark (**photo 5**). Before making your cuts, put a sacrificial piece of wood underneath the workpiece to avoid

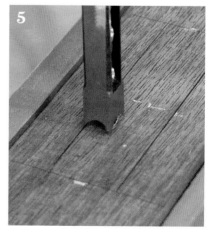

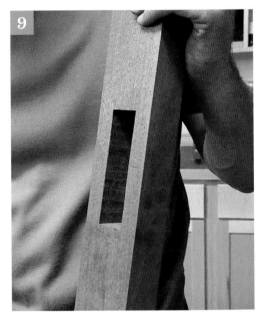

blowout on the backside of your board (**photo 6**). The sacrificial piece provides good insurance any time a mortise goes all the way through the workpiece. Once your piece is in place on the machine, you simply make a series of overlapping holes, nibbling out the waste (**photo 7**).

Clean up the mortises. The mortising machine does the job quickly, but you still have to clean up the insides of the mortises with a chisel. Clamp the workpiece to the bench on top of a sacrificial base that protects the benchtop. Then use a sharp chisel to clean up the rough sides of the mortise (**photo 8**). When you've worked your way all around the mortise, the rough edges left by the mortising machine should

be gone (**photo 9**). Whether you make the mortises by hand or by machine, the inside walls should be relatively smooth once you're done.

T-Mac Tip

For maximum control when cleaning up mortises, hold the chisel securely against your body. Place your thumb against the front of the chisel to stabilize the tool, then push down with your body in a controlled manner.

Finish the joinery by cutting the tenons

Cut the shoulders. This table features shouldered tenons, which are strong and resistant to racking. To cut the shoulders, I remove a little material all the way around the end of the stretcher and the posts (**photo 1**). The tenons go all the way through the mating pieces, with roughly $1/16$ in. of material coming out the other side. The excess will be trimmed away later on.

Set the marking gauge. Start by setting a marking gauge to the thickness of the part with the mortise (**photo 2**). Set the gauge so the blade just kisses the edge of the piece.

Transfer the line. Tighten the gauge and transfer that dimension to the piece to be tenoned (**photo 3**). Mark both faces and both edges, making sure the marking gauge is pressed firmly against the edge of the board (**photo 4**).

Mark the shoulder. The shoulder will be $1/4$ in. wide, so reset the marking gauge to that dimension and make a reference line on the end of the piece. This is how much material you need to remove (**photo 5**).

Set the tablesaw. Put the piece face down on the tablesaw. Raise the dado blades until they are just underneath the shoulder reference line (**photo 6**). Next, move the fence over until the outside blade is lined up with the other reference line (**photo 7**). Now move the fence away from the blade about half the thickness of a tooth. This will allow the tenon to stick out of the mortise slightly.

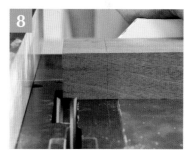

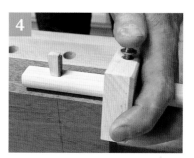
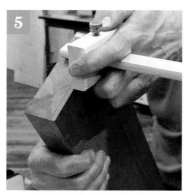

Make the cuts. Make a series of passes over the tablesaw, taking a little material off each time (**photo 8**), then clean up the tenon at the bench with a shoulder plane until you've got a snug fit.

Assembling the base

Flare the mortise. Before putting anything together, the ends of all the mortises should be flared so they are slightly longer on their outside faces. When a wedge is driven into a sawkerf in the end of the tenon, the tenon will spread apart and lock the joint tightly together. Mark the flared ends with a marking knife so the mortise will be roughly ¼ in. longer at each end (**photo 1**). Pare the ends of the mortise down about halfway with a chisel and mallet. You can go a little farther, but take care not to go all the way through (**photo 2**). It doesn't have to be pretty—no one will see it and it will still work perfectly well.

Dry-fit the pieces. Check the fit of all the parts by pushing each tenon into its corresponding mortise. The tenon should go a little bit beyond the opposite face of the piece (**photo 3**). The extra will be trimmed away later on.

Cut the angles on the battens. The battens on this table are tapered. I choose to do this as a design element, but it is optional. I like it because it helps lighten the table visually. If you go this route, make a mark roughly 1 in. up from the bottom of the batten (**photo 4**) and another the same distance out from the post (**photo 5**). Connect the lines (**photo 6**) and cut away the waste. I use a bandsaw for this, but if you don't have one, use a jigsaw or even a handplane.

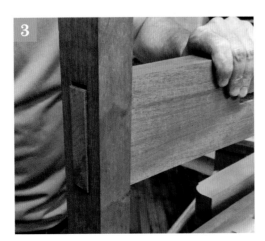

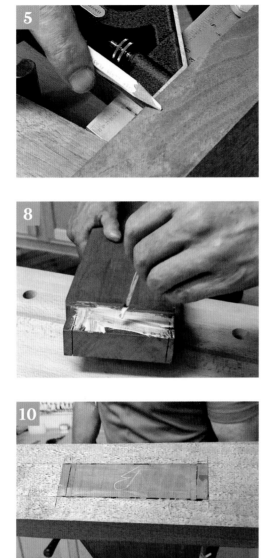

Cut kerfs in the tenon. Each tenon needs a pair of sawkerfs to make room for wedges. I cut about two-thirds of the way down the tenon. The kerfs are ¼ in. to ⅜ in. in from the end **(photo 7)**.

Glue up the pieces. Spread glue on the inside of the mortise and on the tenon. Don't use too much glue—it will just make a mess **(photo 8)**.

Starting with the battens and posts, glue all of the required surfaces and use a deadblow hammer and clamps to seat the batten to the post. Then wedge the

tenon on both sides, alternating from side to side with the mallet making sure the wedges go in evenly **(photo 9)**. After the wedges are in, take the clamps off. The glue will need about an hour or so to set.

Next, flush the post to the battens with a handplane and then connect the trestles together with the stretcher, following the same steps used to connect the battens to the posts. Make sure the base is square when clamping. These joints are ultra strong and will stand up well to the daily abuse a table gets **(photo 10)**.

The feet are square pieces ¾ in. thick and sized to the width of the batten. Just glue them on, making sure the grain of the foot and batten are going in the same direction.

Making a Spring Joint

The top for the trestle table is glued up from several pieces. The key to creating virtually invisible seams between the boards is the spring joint.

Start by clamping two adjacent boards together face to face. Put them in a vise and run a plane down the full length of the boards until the edges are perfectly even with each other **(photo 1)**. Make one pass about 6 in. long at the midway point of the joint, barely taking off any material.

Now come back farther, maybe two-thirds of the way out from the center point, and make another pass **(photo 2).** Then take another pass, starting and ending a little farther than the last pass. The objective here is to make the two meeting edges slightly concave end to end. When the edges are together, you should be able to see a very small gap in the middle, not even $\frac{1}{64}$ in.—just a few shavings wide **(photo 3).**

It only takes very light clamping pressure at the center of the boards to bring the joint tightly together. You won't have to worry about the ends of the joint opening up over time **(photo 4).**

When all of the top pieces have been jointed this way, the boards can be glued together. Spread glue on one edge of each joint and clamp them up. Start by placing one clamp in the middle and then space out additional clamps on either side, keeping them about 12 in. to 16 in. apart until you reach the two ends of the table top. This process ensures that you will have a clean glue joint.

Making the top

Mill the stock. The top starts with rough material just like the base. The top will have to be glued up from two or more pieces, which are milled the same way as the pieces for the base. This means that they are rough milled, allowed to acclimate overnight, and then cut to their finished dimensions the next day. The rough stock for this top was 5/4 in. thick and milled to a finished thickness of 7/8 in.

Glue up the top. Pieces for the top are glued together edge to edge. The edges must be jointed, either on a jointer or by hand with a plane. I use something called a spring joint to get seams that are virtually invisible (see Making a Spring Joint on the facing page).

Make the breadboard ends. Breadboard ends are narrow pieces of perpendicular stock at each end of the top. They're a nice detail visually, and they help keep the tabletop flat (**photo 1**). Start by cutting a 1/4-in. by 3/16-in. groove in the center of each breadboard piece and then cut a series of 3/4-in. mortises down the length of the groove (**photo 2**). Leave about 1 in. of material between the mortises. If you don't do this, the breadboard pieces will be very weak.

Cut tenons on the ends of the top to fit the groove and the mortises. The mortises closest to the outside edges of the top should be a little wider than the tenons to allow the top to shrink and expand seasonally. Giving the tenons some breathing room guarantees the top won't crack or buckle. For the same reason, when you glue on the breadboard ends, glue the middle tenons but not the ones on the outside.

T-Mac tip

Make the breadboard ends slightly thicker than the boards for the top. After the top is assembled, use a handplane to flush up the two surfaces.

Apply finish. After touching up the breadboard ends with a handplane and sanding all of the surfaces of the frame and top, the table is ready for finish (**photo 3**). My favorite finish is linseed oil followed by blond shellac and wax, which brings out the deep luster and natural color of the walnut. For details on finishing, see pp. 162–181.

WALL CABINET

TECHNIQUE

Creating Moldings

A wall cabinet is a great way to show off some special wood, like the crotch-grained black walnut I used for this project. A cabinet of this size doesn't require too much time or too many materials to build. It's an ideal project that can be made in a weekend or two.

The case is fairly simple, just four boards joined at the corners with half-blind dovetails and a single shelf secured by dadoes cut into the sides of the case. The back is made of two shiplapped boards screwed into a rabbet.

The most dominant feature is the molding. It's built up in three layers, beginning with a band of dentil molding that's easy to make on a tablesaw (see Build Your Skills on p. 40). The two other profiles are produced on a router table. Together, they provide an elegant feature with lots of shadow lines and detail.

The use of built-up moldings on furni-ture mirrors the kind of ornate architectural trim seen on buildings around the world. This project takes its inspiration from the Old North Church in Boston, a church that played an important role in the American Revolution (visit the church in the Road Trip sidebar on p. 38). Borrowing historical details like this is a time-honored tradition among furniture makers.

Although this wall cabinet gets a lot of its character from the walnut, it could be built from just about any type of wood, including cherry, mahogany, or other species that aren't as pricey, like pine and ash. In the end, it will be just as functional and pleasing to the eye.

Wall Cabinet

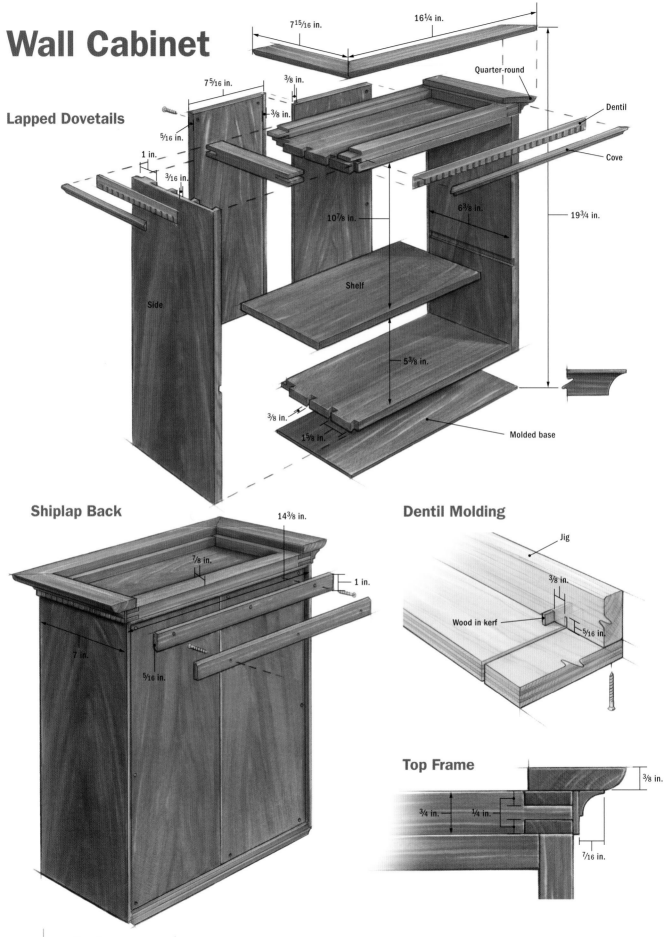

Lapped Dovetails

7 15/16 in.

16 1/4 in.

Quarter-round

7 5/16 in.

3/8 in.

3/8 in.

Dentil

5/16 in.

Cove

1 in.

3/16 in.

6 3/8 in.

19 3/4 in.

10 7/8 in.

Shelf

Side

5 3/8 in.

3/8 in.

Molded base

1 5/8 in.

Shiplap Back

14 3/8 in.

7/8 in.

1 in.

7 in.

5/16 in.

Dentil Molding

Jig

3/8 in.

Wood in kerf

5/16 in.

Top Frame

3/8 in.

3/4 in.   1/4 in.

7/16 in.

MATERIALS LIST/ROUGH MILL

PART	# OF PIECES	LENGTH (IN.)	WIDTH (IN.)	THICKNESS (IN.)	WOOD	NOTES
Sides	2	19	7½	¾	Primary	
Top & bottom	2	15	6⅞	¾	Primary	
Shelf	1	14⅜	6⅞	⅝	Primary	
Frame front & back	2	15⅜	1⅜	⅞	Primary	
Frame sides	2	8	1⅜	⅞	Primary	
Dentil front	1	15⅝	⅞	1	Primary	
Dentil sides	2	8	⅞	1	Primary	
Quarter-round front	1	17¼	2½	½	Primary	
Quarter-round sides	2	15¹⁵⁄₁₆	2½	½	Primary	
Cove front	1	16½	1	⁹⁄₁₆	Primary	
Cove sides	2	8⁹⁄₁₆	1	⁹⁄₁₆	Primary	
Molded bottom	1	15³⁄₁₆	7⅜	¾	Primary	
Shiplap back	2	19	15¹³⁄₁₆	⁷⁄₁₆	Primary	
French cleat	2	15	1½	⁷⁄₁₆	Primary	
Screws	4					#6 × 1-in. flat head
Screws	8					#6 × ⅝-in. flat head
Screws	2					#8 × 1½-in. flat head

Rough dimensions are slightly longer, wider and thicker than the finished dimensions. Mill the stock, sticker it overnight, and then bring pieces to the finished dimensions the following day.

TOOLS

POWER TOOLS
Bandsaw
Cordless drill
Jointer
Miter saw
Mortising machine
Planer
Router table
Tablesaw with
  dado blade

HAND TOOLS
Chisels
Clamps
Dovetail saw
Handplane
Marking gauge

Making the case

I made the case for this cabinet from flitches of walnut cut and stacked sequentially so I'd get a good grain and color match **(photo 1).** The crotch grain, where two parts of the trunk or a trunk and a branch come together, is what inspired me. So I marked out the best areas of the boards with chalk before cutting out the pieces **(photo 2).** Sections

of straight-grained material were perfect for making the moldings.

Rough-mill the pieces. As always, start by cutting pieces slightly larger than their finished dimensions (1 in. longer in length, $^1/_2$ in. more in width, and $^1/_8$ in. to $^3/_{16}$ in. greater in thickness), stickering them overnight, and bringing them to their finished dimensions the following day.

Cut the half-blind dovetails. The sides are joined to the top and bottom of the case with half-blind dovetails **(photo 3).** This joint makes a very strong box. Unlike through-dovetails, half-blind dovetails are not intended to be a decorative detail because they'll never be seen.

Mark the rabbets. With the box assembled (without glue), mark the location of the rabbets on the back of the case with chalk **(photo 4).** That's an easy way to avoid mixing up the pieces at the tablesaw and making the cuts in the wrong place—not a hard thing to do.

Set up the dado blade. Take the box apart and stack the pieces on the tablesaw so all of the marked edges are oriented the same way **(photo 5).** Stack the dado so it's $^3/_4$ in. wide, and set the height of the cut at $^3/_8$ in. **(photo 6).** The width of the rabbet must accommodate the back pieces as well as a French cleat that will be used to hang the cabinet.

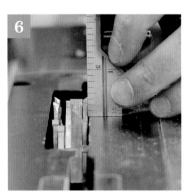

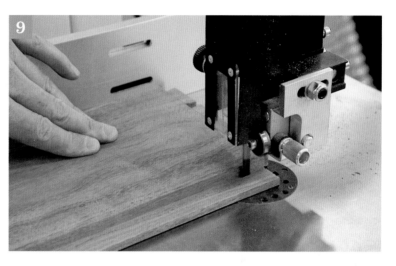

Attach a sacrificial fence.
To avoid doing any damage to the
manufactured fence, clamp a piece of
medium-density fiberboard (MDF) or
plywood to the fence and move the fence
over so it's just touching the innermost
tooth of the blade (**photo 7**).

Cut the rabbets. After testing the
setup on a piece of scrap, run the four
pieces of the case over the blade and cut
the rabbets (**photo 8**).

Cut the shelf dadoes. Change
the dado set to a width of $^1/_2$ in. and set
the height at $^3/_{16}$ in. Placement of the shelf
isn't crucial. For this project I measured
6 in. up from the bottom of the case. This
design provides one large and one small
storage area in the finished piece.

T-Mac Tip

If you're nervous
about the stock
riding on the
miter gauge and
the fence at the
same time, clamp a block on the fence as
shown. The block will locate the workpiece
correctly for the cut but won't be in contact
during the cut, eliminating the chance that
the workpiece will bind.

Trim the top and bottom pieces.
Before the case can be assembled, the
rabbet on the top and bottom pieces
should be cut away. This gives the back
pieces a wider place for attachment. You
make the cuts on a bandsaw and then
clean them up with a handplane (**photo
9**). Now sand the inside of the case with
150-grit paper and glue the case together.

Glossary

A **dado set** is a
stack of cutters
that replaces a
conventional blade
on the tablesaw.
Blades can be
combined in different
ways, with or without
shims, to produce
dadoes and rabbets
of different widths.

Letting History Be the Guide

Molding details in furniture often come from the architectural details found on historic buildings, and there's no better place to find inspiration than the Old North Church in Boston, which dates from 1723 (photo left). Lanterns were hung from its steeple "one if by land, and two if by sea," to warn Colonists of the British approach at the dawn of the American Revolution.

The outside of the church is simple brick, but the beautiful moldings that encircle the upper reaches of the building add to its character. The layered bands of molding are just as evident inside as they are outside (see the photo below left).

Period furniture maker Phil Lowe showed an example of how layered moldings in similar profiles can be used, in this case on a reproduction Philadelphia highboy originally dating from 1750 (see the top photo below).

Back then, furniture makers would have used wooden planes to create the molding profiles, as Phil demonstrates in the bottom photo below. These days, we can get nearly the same results using router bits and shaper cutterheads.

Old North Church

Layered moldings on reproduction furniture

Molding details on the Old North Church in Boston

Creating molding profiles with a wooden plane

Making the top frame

At the top of the case is a simple frame that's ³/₄ in. thick. The frame provides a separate surface from the box on which to attach the moldings. This also allows for proper glue surface and seasonal movement for the case. The corners of the frame are joined with slip joints, which are basically open-ended mortise-and-tenon joints (**photo 1**). They can be made with a router, a mortising machine, or even by hand; In this instance I used a tablesaw.

Use a zero-clearance insert. Since pieces for the frame are relatively small, added precautions are needed at the tablesaw. Dropping in a zero-clearance insert will help to prevent any problems (**photo 2**).

Set up the dado blade. Use a ¼-in.-wide dado blade to make the mortises. Set up the fence so the mortise will be centered in the stock. The height of the blade is set to just below the width of the frame pieces. This will leave a little extra material on the edges of the frame that will be trimmed later so the frame ends up being flush to the box.

Use a backer block. To run such small pieces of material over the saw safely, position a backer block directly behind the piece for greater stability. Keep both the piece and the backer block tight against the fence when making each cut (**photo 3**). Remember when making the cuts to push both the piece and block well past the insert before removing.

Now cut the tenons. Adjust the height of the blade so it equals one side of the mortised piece (**photo 4**), and make the tenons in a series of passes over the blade. Use a backer block that rides against the fence, but cut a groove in the block before you start making the tenons (**photo 5**).

Glue up and attach the frame. Glue the frame together, trim it to size, and then attach it to the case by gluing the front edge and screwing the sides near the back. Elongate the two screw holes by drilling a pilot hole and then moving the bit in an arc. This allows the screw to pivot slightly as the top of the box shrinks and expands seasonally.

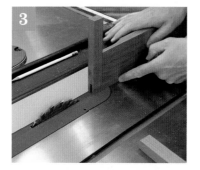

Making Dentil Moldings

The dentil molding for this cabinet is made from strips of wood cut from a blank called a log **(photo 1)**.

First, joint one edge of the log with a plane or on a jointer, and then rip several ⅛-in.-thick strips on the tablesaw, making extras as backup **(photo 2)**. Be sure to plane the edge of the log in between each rip to ensure the face of the molding will be free of mill marks.

The molding is cut on a jig that's basically a length of scrap (longer than the length of your ripped pieces) with two sawkerfs cut in one edge. The distance between the kerfs (slots) equals the width of each tooth of the molding. I space the teeth ⅜ in. apart **(photo 3)**. After cutting the two slots, insert a piece of material equal to the width of the kerf into one of the slots so one end protrudes slightly.

Next, screw a piece of plywood to the bottom of the jig to provide a stable base for the molding.

The first slot in the molding is made with the end of the blank against the index piece **(photo 4)**. After that, it's just a matter of dropping that slot over the index piece and making another cut **(photo 5)**. Just work your way down the blank until each strip of molding is complete. Remember to push the molding strip completely past the blade and remove it from the jig each time before pulling the jig back over the blade.

T-Mac Tip

If the back of the molding shows any tearout, try using a backer piece directly behind the molding, as shown.

Finishing the molding

In addition to the dentil molding, there are two other profiles: a cove and a roundover. Both are cut on the router table, a machine to be extra careful around.

Cut the cap piece profile with a quarter-round bit. This is the molding at the very top of the case, which is $1/2$ in. thick and $1^7/8$ in. wide. It's made with a $3/4$-in. quarter-round bit in several passes. Don't try to take all of the material off in a single pass; it may overtax the router and the cut won't be as clean **(photo 1)**. If you have a split fence on your router table, close the two sides in so they are close to the bit, which will reduce tearout.

Cut the profile to width. After routing the profile along one edge, cut the molding to the correct width on the tablesaw. I made these pieces $1^7/8$ in. wide.

Cut the cove. Change the bit in the router table to a $1/2$-in. cove bit **(photo 2)**. Start with stock that's $2^1/2$ in. wide, cut the profile in one edge, and then rip the profiled edge off at the tablesaw **(photo 3)**. These are ripped to a width of $3/8$ in.

Profile the bottom. The bottom piece is a $5/8$-in.-thick board that's profiled on the front and two side edges and glued to the bottom of the case. These cove cuts are also made on the router table. Cut the sides first, then the front. If the crossgrain side cuts cause any tearout, the long-grain pass will clean it up **(photo 4)**.

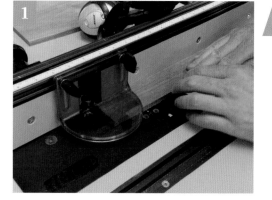

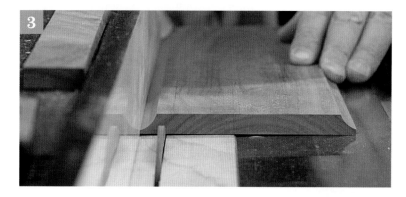

Safety First

Router bits are sharp, and they turn at very high speeds. Make sure you keep fingers well clear of the bit when the router is running.

Safety First

Always unplug any power tool before changing bits.

Applying the molding

The molding at the top of the case is applied in three layers: first the strip of dentil, then the cap pieces, and finally the cove. Start by trimming the sides of the frame on top of the case with a plane so all sides are flush.

Start with the dentil. Place the cabinet on the bench, face up, and cut a piece of dentil for the front. The ends should overhang the sides by the thickness of the strip, plus a small allowance that will be trimmed later **(photo 1).** Run a bead of glue on the back of the dentil (not too much!), lightly dab the ends of all the teeth, and clamp the strip in place **(photo 2).** Then cut and add the dentil on the sides of the case, gluing and clamping following the same process.

Cut the cap pieces. The cap pieces are mitered at the front corners and cut square at the back. Start with the front piece, cutting a 45-degree miter at one end. Use a backup piece on the miter saw to reduce tearout **(photo 3).** Cut a miter on one end of a side piece, mark the length from the case, and then make that cut on the miter saw. Dry-fit those two pieces on the case to make sure the miter is tight.

Glue and screw the cap pieces. Drill two pilot holes in the side piece, add a bead of glue, and screw the piece into place. Make sure the back edge of the molding is flush with the back of the case. Mark the length of the front piece directly from the case **(photo 4),** cut it to length, and glue and screw that down. Then cut and add the other side piece, making whatever adjustments are necessary in the miter to get a tight fit.

Add the cove. The cove is applied last, glued and clamped directly beneath the cap piece and over the dentil **(photo 5).** A piece of Styrofoam® can be used as a caul. It molds to the irregular shape and allows for better clamping pressure.

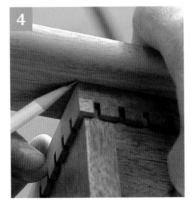

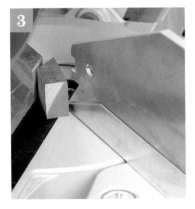

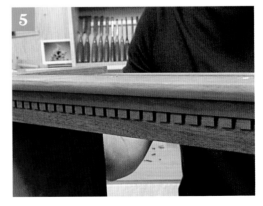

Adding the back, bottom, and cleat

The back of the case is made of two solid boards ⁵/₁₆ in. thick that overlap in the middle with a shiplap joint (**photo 1**). This joint allows for seasonal movement in the wood and prevents the back pieces from cracking.

Size the back pieces. Cut two pieces for the back so their total width is slightly less than the opening. An allowance of ¹/₈ in. is about right.

Machine the shiplap. Using a ¹/₂-in.-wide dado blade on the tablesaw, cut a rabbet on one long edge of each back board, removing half the thickness of each board to create the shiplap.

Screw in the back. Predrill and countersink two holes at the corners on the long edges of each board, plus one at the center, and drill one additional hole at the top and bottom of the overlapping board. Then drill pilot holes in the case, and attach both pieces with #6 by ⁵/₈-in. screws. The outside edges of the back pieces should fit tightly against the case (**photo 2**). The gap between the boards at the back of the case is a practical necessity for wood movement, but it also makes a nice detail (**photo 3**).

Add the bottom. Glue and clamp the profiled board to the bottom of the case (**photo 4**). Because the board is cut smaller than the case, there will be a ³/₃₂-in. reveal between the board and the bottom along the front and the sides. The back edge of the board should be flush with the back of the case. When the case is hung on the wall, the bottom hides the half-blind dovetails and helps make the case look completely finished (**photo 5**).

Make the French cleat. Cut two pieces of stock ⁵/₁₆ in. thick to a length that fits across the back of the case inside the rabbet. Then make a 30-degree bevel along one edge of each piece (**photo 6**). Screw one piece to the top at the back of the case, right below the frame. Make sure the screws are going into the top of the box and not just through the backboards. Orient the cleat so the point of the bevel is toward the back (**photo 7**). The two edges of the cleats interlock, which keeps the cabinet firmly in place and flat against the wall.

OCTAGONAL LAZY SUSAN

Creating a Veneer Inlay

The most common style of lazy Susan is made with a plain round top that turns on a base. This project goes a step further with its octagonal shape and veneered inlaid pattern.

The tablesaw is an important tool for this project. With proper techniques and simple jigs, it precisely cuts both the eight-sided top and the circular base (learn how to do this in Build Your Skills on pp. 50–51).

The veneer inlay on the walnut top gives the project a distinctive look. The octagonal pattern is composed of two contrasting veneers, bird's-eye maple and bee's-wing mahogany, that really pop out of the black walnut. Although it may look complicated, the pattern is made with simple tools and techniques.

The inspiration for the inlay pattern comes from a Federal-style bookcase dating from about 1800. For a look at some of those period details, I visited Historic New England's Collections and Conservation Center (see more in the Road Trip sidebar on p. 52).

A lazy Susan is a manageable project that doesn't require a lot of material, and the inlay is a great introduction to working with veneer. Different kinds of wood can be substituted for the top, base, and veneers; and no matter what you choose, the result will be practical and beautiful.

Lazy Susan

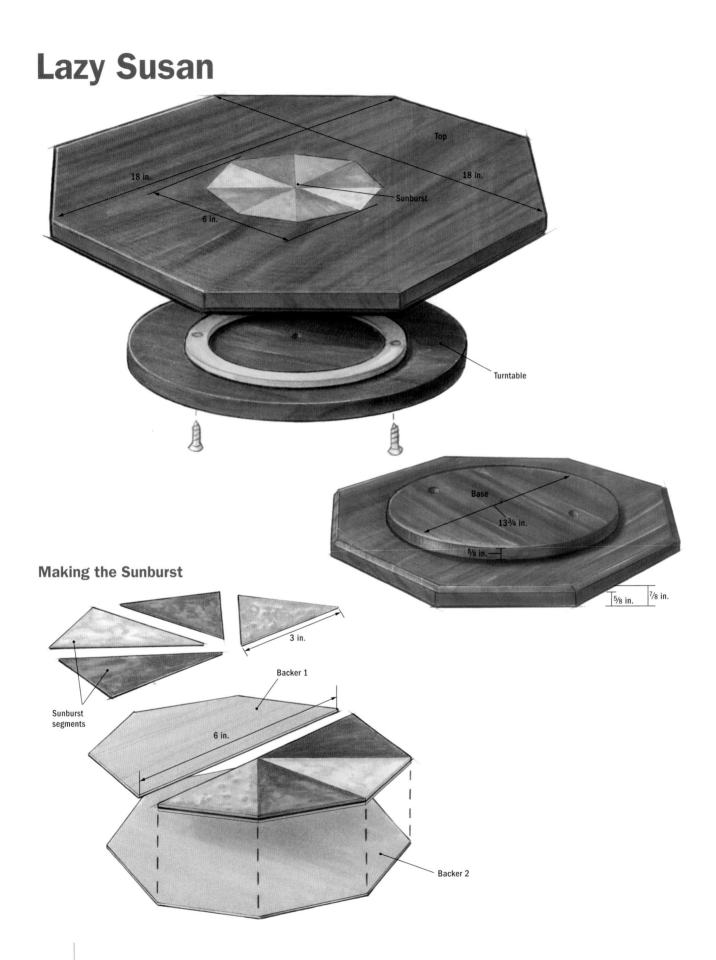

Top

18 in.

18 in.

Sunburst

6 in.

Turntable

Base

13¾ in.

⅝ in.

⅝ in.   ⅞ in.

Making the Sunburst

3 in.

Sunburst segments

Backer 1

6 in.

Backer 2

MATERIALS LIST/ROUGH MILL

PART	# OF PIECES	LENGTH (IN.)	WIDTH (IN.)	THICKNESS (IN.)	WOOD	NOTES
Top	1	19	19	1	Primary	
Base	1	14¾	14¾	¾	Primary	
Sunburst veneer 1	1				1 sq. ft; bird's-eye maple	
Sunburst veneer 2	1				1 sq. ft; bee's-wing mahogany	
Backer veneer	2				1 sq. ft.; backer	
Screws	8					#6 × ½ in.
Lazy Susan hardware	1					

Rough dimensions are slightly longer, wider and thicker than finished dimensions. Mill the stock, sticker it overnight, and then bring pieces to the finished dimensions the following day.

Making the top

The top starts with a rough board of black walnut that should be at least 19 in. by 19 in. and milled before it's cut to shape. Not every shop will have a jointer or planer big enough to handle material this wide, so here's a chance to put your bench planes to good use and get a little cardio going in the process. You'll also want to make sure your plane irons are razor sharp before you get down to work (see pp. 10–11 for how to sharpen a plane).

Mark the thickness. Flatten one face of the board, then use a marking gauge to scribe a line ⅞ in. from the face on all four edges **(photo 1).** Plane the board to the right thickness. The board should measure slightly more than 18 in. sq. when you're done.

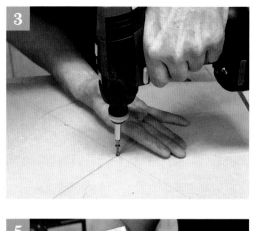

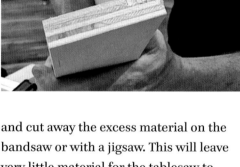

Make the pattern. You need only one simple pattern to cut the octagonal top. The pattern is made from ¹/₂-in. or ³/₄-in. medium-density fiberboard (MDF) or plywood that's exactly 18 in. sq. Draw two diagonal lines from corner to corner and drill a hole through the pattern where the lines intersect. Drill a second hole roughly 6 in. out from the center along one of the lines (**photo 2**). Placement of the second hole isn't crucial.

Attach the pattern. Once you've milled what will become the finished top, decide which side will be the face of your project. Mark the front and back accordingly. The pattern should be attached with screws to the bottom of the project (**photo 3**).

Trim the top to size. Draw a line that is roughly ¹/₈ in. away from the edge of the pattern on all four sides (**photo 4**),

and cut away the excess material on the bandsaw or with a jigsaw. This will leave very little material for the tablesaw to remove.

Make an L-fence. To cut the top on the tablesaw, you'll need an L-fence. To make an L-fence you'll need two pieces of ³/₄-in. plywood that are about 3 in. wide and 30 in. long. Cut a ³/₄-in. wide dado ¹/₄ in. deep and ³/₈ in. off the bottom of one piece of plywood. Glue and screw the other piece of plywood into the dado (**photo 5**).

Set up the saw. Clamp the L-fence to your rip fence so that it's about ³/₁₆ in. higher than the thickness of the top. The offcuts from trimming the sides of the top at the bandsaw make for a good gauge (**photo 6**). Then set the height of the blade so that it's high enough to cut all the way through the top. Adjust the fence so

the leading edge of the L-fence overhangs the blade slightly (**photo 7**).

Trim the top. Run all four edges of the pattern against the L-fence, trimming away the waste and creating a perfectly square piece (**photo 8**).

Rotate the pattern. Back out the screw that prevented the pattern from rotating (not the one at the center), turn the pattern 45 degrees, and drive the screw back into the bottom using the same hole in the pattern (**photo 9**).

Finish the cuts. Cut away the excess material outside the pattern using a jigsaw or bandsaw. Return to the tablesaw and flush-cut the other four sides (still using the L-fence) to complete the octagonal shape (**photo 10**).

Chamfer the bottom edge. To lighten the look of the top, cut a ¼-in. by ¼-in. 45-degree chamfer on the bottom edge. Using the tablesaw, tilt the blade to 45 degrees and set the blade height to ¼ in. Move the rip fence to the other side of the blade so the teeth are leaning toward the fence. Position and attach the L-fence just above the blade and cut all eight sides, creating a chamfer (**photo 11**). When you're done at the tablesaw, remove the mill marks from all the edges. This can be done back at the bench with a vise and bench plane. And remember—always go with the grain.

Cutting a Perfect Circle on the Tablesaw

The circular base is just a little smaller than the octagonal top. Although the base could be cut using a jigsaw, a bandsaw, or a router, I wanted to share a trick I learned from my high school shop teacher that's done at the tablesaw.

To create the base, make a 13½-in.-sq. piece of stock ½ in. thick. You could even use a piece of plywood or scraps from around the shop. Find the center of the board and draw the biggest circle that you possibly can using a set of trammel points **(photo 1)**. If you don't have a set, just use a pencil and a piece of string or dental floss **(photo 2)**. Rough out the circle on a bandsaw or a jigsaw, making sure you stay just outside of the line. Then drill a small hole (which you

Safety First

Remember to rotate the base piece counterclockwise, against the rotation of the blade, and always keep firm pressure on the base.

previously marked) through the center of the base.

From one edge of a piece of ¾-in. plywood, measure inward a distance equal to the radius of the base less ⅛ in. Drill and countersink a hole at that spot **(photo 3)**. Put a screw through the hole you've just drilled, insert the tip of the screw into the center hole of the base, and screw the two pieces together **(photo 4)**. The edge of the base should stick out just past the edge of the plywood pattern.

Place the plywood on the tablesaw and position it so the edge of the base piece covers about half the thickness of the tablesaw blade—about ³⁄₃₂ in. or so

(photo 5). Clamp the plywood firmly to the table. For now, make sure the teeth are not in contact with the edge of the base piece.

Finally, hold the base piece down firmly with one hand, turn on the saw, and, very slowly, crank up the blade until it starts to cut the base piece—⅛ in. to ³⁄₁₆ in. deep. Rotate the piece a full revolution **(photo 6)** and adjust the blade up another ⅛ in. to ³⁄₁₆ in. and make another full revolution. Continue to adjust the blade up after each pass until the circle has been cut completely.

Inspired by an Old Idea

Inlaid veneers
on Federal-style
bookcase

Federal-style bookcase
joined to Chippendale
desk

The veneer pattern decorating the center of the lazy Susan is similar to a detail in a 200-year-old piece of furniture that we found at Historic New England's Collections and Conservation Center in Haverhill, Massachusetts (see the top photo at left).

Inlaid veneers were prominent in furniture made during the Federal period. The bookcase portion of this piece features a veneered oval in the pediment as well as veneered fans in the corners of the two doors. The bookcase was made around 1800. What makes the piece really interesting is that it's joined to a

Chippendale-style desk that was made some 20 years earlier (see the bottom photo at left).

While the bookcase is all about veneer, the desk features carved details in solid wood, a classic characteristic of Chippendale furniture (see the top center photo below). These features were also seen in other examples of Chippendale furniture in the Conservation Center's huge collection, including a chest with intricately carved knees (see the bottom center photo below) and another piece with a fan carved into an upper drawer (see the bottom right photo).

While details like these help define older furniture styles, they also can be applied to more contemporary work, which is the case with our lazy Susan. Also worth noting is the fact that the process for creating those details has changed very little over the last 200 years.

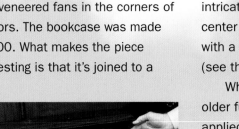

Carved details (photos above) in Chippendale desk

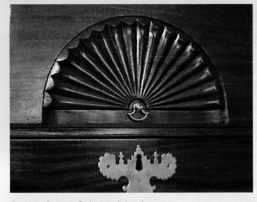

Carved fan on Chippendale chest

Attaching the base

The base and top are connected with a turntable made of two interlocking pieces of steel that rotate smoothly on ball bearings. The turntables are widely available at woodworking stores. They come in various sizes; the one I used is 12 in. in diameter.

Lay out the hardware location. Draw a circle on the top of the base piece with a diameter equal to the inside diameter of the turntable. Center the turntable on the circle and screw it down (**photo 1**).

Mark the hole locations. Trace the outlines of the two large access holes on the base (**photo 2**), back out the screws, and remove the turntable.

Drill the access holes. Using a ³/₄-in. or ⁷/₈-in. Forstner bit, drill out the access holes at the locations you've just marked. Put a piece of scrap under the workpiece so you won't damage your bench (**photo 3**).

Attach the turntable. Draw a circle with the same diameter as the inside of the turntable on the bottom of the octagonal top. Then flip the turntable over and center it on the circle. Drive two screws into the base through the holes in the turntable (**photo 4**), then back out the screws and remove the turntable. These holes will allow the turntable to be located correctly later on. Now, reattach the turntable to the base piece. Flip the base piece and turntable over, place them on the bottom of the octagonal top, and use the access holes to find the two index holes you drilled previously (**photo 5**). Drive in those two screws, then spin the base piece so the access holes are exposed driving in the screws as you work your way, around the turntable.

T-Mac Tip

When attaching the turntable to the base, start all of the screws in their predrilled holes before driving any of them down tightly. It will make it easier to reposition the turntable if you have to.

Making the veneered pattern

The sunburst at the center of the lazy Susan is made from alternating triangles of bee's-wing mahogany and bird's-eye maple. The pieces are cut from sheets of veneer, edge-jointed in pairs, and glued to a backer piece of mahogany veneer.

Treat the veneer. Wood veneer is only 1/42 in. thick, and when it gets to your shop it's likely to be very brittle. The first step is to spray each piece of veneer with veneer softener (**photo 1**) (you can buy it premixed or you can make your own) and stack the pieces sequentially with a piece of newspaper between each sheet. The cluster of veneers should then be sandwiched together between two pieces of plywood or MDF, clamped, and allowed to sit overnight. The next day swap out the wet newspaper with sheets of dry paper

p
by
an
of (
The
a 6-
dista
point
to an (
sions y   .. the triangles on
the veneer.

Cut out the triangles. First cut out the triangles from the graph paper, then lay them on pieces of mahogany and maple veneer, making them slightly over-size so you have extra material for fitting. Make an X on each face piece so all the pieces will have the same face showing. Next, cut out the triangles with a scalpel or sharp knife (**photo 3**). Cut a few extra of each type of veneer.

Lay out the pattern on the bench. Take the triangles you've just cut and arrange them in a pattern on the bench. Inspect the pieces carefully, and discard any with flaws or discolorations (**photo 4**). When you're happy with the

layout, number the pieces to help keep them organized (**photo 5**).

Make a shooting board. The pieces will be jointed using a shooting board, which is easy to make from a few scraps of MDF. It consists of a base piece and an arm that swings on a pivot (**photo 6**). Use one of the triangles to find the angle of the arm (which should be $22\frac{1}{2}$ degrees plus a margin of $\frac{1}{4}$ degree more) and then clamp the arm in place.

Shoot the edges in pairs. Take adjoining pairs of triangles and fold them together face to face, then place the pieces together on the shooting board (**photo 7**). Use a bench plane on its side to joint the two edges simultaneously, just as you would joint the edges of boards you were gluing up (**photo 8**). Make very light cuts until the plane is no longer removing any veneer.

Test the fit. Unfold the pieces and place them together on the bench. Check that the edges line up, without any gaps, and then come together making a perfect point (**photo 9**). Using this same process, work your way around the pattern until you've shot all the edges.

Tape the pieces together. The pieces are joined, face side up, a pair at a time, with veneer tape. Wipe the glue side of the tape with a dampened cloth or paper towel, hold the pieces tightly, and then tape them together. Concentrate on the tips to make sure they're aligned (**photo 10**). Make two sections, each consisting of four triangles, and glue each half (using yellow or cold-press glue) to a backer piece of mahogany veneer that's cut roughly to shape. Spread the glue evenly to cover the veneer completely without going overboard. Then clamp the

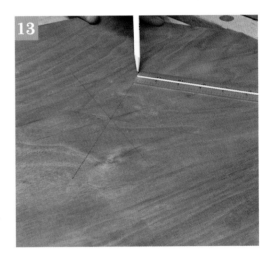

veneer between two pieces of MDF or plywood and allow it to dry for at least 45 minutes (read the drying instructions on the back of your glue of choice).

T-Mac Tip

When gluing the assembled triangles to the backer piece, make sure to use waxed paper between the veneer and the plywood or MDF so they won't stick together.

Trim the pieces. Once the glue has dried, place one half of the pattern on the shooting board and shoot the long edge with a plane (**photo 11**). Repeat with the other half. Keep an eye on where the tips meet and make absolutely sure you don't plane past the points, just up to them.

Join the halves together. When each half pattern has been jointed, position them face up and tape them together, paying close attention to the center points of each of the two halves so they match perfectly. Take the newly formed pattern and glue it to another piece of mahogany veneer. After the glue is dry, dampen the veneer tape, which will reactivate the glue and make the removal of the tape easier. Sometimes using a card scraper can make the job less stressful.

Cut the edges. The outside edges of the pattern still need to be trimmed. Measure out from the center 3 in. at each point where the triangles are joined, and cut away the excess with a straightedge and sharp knife (**photo 12**). Make light strokes and multiples passes to cut through the three layers of veneer.

Lay out the pattern location. Find the center point of the top. Using an adjustable square, draw four intersecting lines (**photo 13**) that cross in the center. Lay the pattern on the top and line up each point of the octagon to land on the pencil lines. Trace around the outside of the pattern with a knife or a pencil. Make an indexing mark both on the pattern and on the top so when you move the pieces around you can reorient them again the same way.

Make the recess. I use a plunge router to take out most of the material that will create the recess. Set the depth of cut just slightly more than the thickness of the pattern. Start making the recess, working out from the center of the top so the base of the router is always supported (**photo 14**). Get as close to the lines of the pattern as you're comfortable with. To complete the recess, you need to do some final cleanup of the edges using a sharp chisel. The goal is to have the pattern fit snugly into the recess on all eight sides (**photo 15**).

Glue in the pattern. Start by making a caul out of plywood or MDF that is slightly smaller then your pattern. Next, apply a thin even coat of glue into the recess followed by the pattern and then a piece of wax paper. To apply pressure,

center the caul precisely over the pattern, then clamp into place and allow the glue to dry (**photo 16**).

Sand and finish. Once the glue has dried, methodically sand the top until the veneer pattern and the walnut are completely flush (**photo 17**). Whether you use a power sander or a piece of sandpaper and a block, make sure you don't burn through the thin pieces of veneer in your pattern. Once the surface is completely sanded, the lazy Susan is ready for the finish of your choice.

KEEPSAKE BOX

Reinforcing Miter Joints with Splines

This keepsake box requires only a small amount of material, making it a good project for that short length of special lumber you've been saving. Construction is straightforward, with mitered corners cut on the tablesaw and reinforced with full-length splines (learn how in Build Your Skills on p. 66).

The design of the top, the focal point of this project, is adapted from a desk that once belonged to John Adams (see my Road Trip to the President's home on p. 64). The pattern looks complex, but it's simple to assemble from strips of book-matched veneer, which I made right in the shop from pieces of scrap material. Best of all, the process doesn't require any special tools.

Rather than make a separate box and lid and face the challenge of trying to fit them together, I make this box as a single unit and slice off the top on the tablesaw when it's complete. To keep the top aligned when the box is closed, a lip is applied around the inside edge.

I chose to make the box from butternut, which is an easy-to-work hardwood. It contrasts nicely with the black walnut veneer on top and the black walnut beading inside the lid. This is a great project that can be built in a weekend or two with limited materials. It will also demystify the process of veneering the top.

Keepsake Box

Top and Bottom Panels

$3/16$ in.

Top, $1/2$ in. thick

$1/4$ in.

Inside top

$1\frac{1}{2}$ in.

Grooves

Lip is $3/8$ in. high and $3/16$ in. thick.

$4\frac{1}{2}$ in.

$9\frac{3}{8}$ in.

$12\frac{3}{8}$ in.

Box front

10 in.

Rabbet

Bottom, $1/2$ in. thick

Spline

13 in.

Edges and Triangles

Cross veneer

Centerline

Herringbone veneer

Lid front

$9/16$ in.

$1\frac{5}{16}$ in.

Miters

$1/8$ in.

10 in.

13 in.

$1/8$ in.

$1/4$ in.

Triangle

Spline

Rabbet, $1/8$ in. x $1/8$ in.

Corner bead, $1/8$ in. x $1/8$ in.

Grooves

$1/4$ in.

$1/2$ in.

$3/16$ in.

$1/4$ in.

MATERIALS LIST/ROUGH MILL

PART	# OF PIECES	LENGTH (IN.)	WIDTH (IN.)	THICKNESS (IN.)	WOOD	NOTES
Box front & back	2	14	6⅛	⅝	Primary 1	
Lid front & back	2	14	6⅛	⅝	Primary 1	
Box sides	2	11	6⅛	⅝	Primary 1	
Lid sides	2	11	6⅛	⅝	Primary 1	
Splines	1	Long enough for milling	6½	¼	Primary 1	
Herringbone veneer	1	10¾	1¹³⁄₁₆	2	Primary 2	
Cross veneer	1	Long enough for milling	10¼	2	Primary 2	
Triangle veneer	2	12	1¹³⁄₁₆	2	Primary 2	
Corner bead edging, long	2	14	⅝	¼	Primary 1	
Corner bead edging, short	2	11	⅝	¼	Primary 1	
Lip, long	2	13⅜	⅞	⁵⁄₁₆	Primary 2	
Lip, short	2	10⅜	⅞	⁵⁄₁₆	Primary 2	
Hinges	2					Box hinges with screws
Latch	1					Latch, clasp, or handle
½-in. Baltic birch plywood for top and bottom	2			½		Measure case at dry-fit

Rough dimensions are slightly longer, wider and thicker than finished dimensions. Mill the stock, sticker it overnight, and then bring pieces to the finished dimensions the following day.

TOOL LIST

POWER TOOLS
Bandsaw
Circular saw or miter saw
In-line sander
Jointer
Planer
Tablesaw with dado blade

HAND TOOLS
Card scraper
Chisels
Clamps
Combination square
Handplane
Marking knife
Miter gauge
Veneer tape

Making the box

The box can be made out of standard 4/4 material, but this one was made using 8/4 stock, which allows for a continuous grain pattern on the outside faces of the box. Start by cutting a kerf lengthwise in both edges of the stock on the tablesaw, then finish the cut on a bandsaw to produce two book-matched pieces (**photo 1**). You then have to reflatten the pieces on a jointer and send them through the thickness planer.

Fold and mark the stock. Fold the two pieces together so the faces you've just sawn are on the outside (**photo 2**). Mark the rough lengths of the side pieces (finished dimension plus 1 in.) on the top edge, laying them out so that when the pieces are assembled into the shape of a box, the grain will flow continuously from one side to the next (**photo 3**). Once you've done this,

mark the outside faces indicating grain direction.

Make the cuts. Cut the pieces to length on a miter saw or with a circular saw (**photo 4**), sticker them overnight, and then mill them to their finished dimensions on the following day. You'll be able to see how well the grain matches when the pieces are lined up in the order in which they will be assembled (**photo 5**).

Add clamping blocks. From scrap, cut eight clamping blocks, each with a 45-degree bevel on one edge. Next, glue the blocks flush to the ends of the side pieces on the outside faces (**photo 6**). The blocks will help you clamp the box together and will serve as a reference point when cutting the miters in the box sides.

Cut pieces to length. At the tablesaw, make sure the blade is at 90 degrees and the miter gauge is square to the blade. Next, set the blade so it is

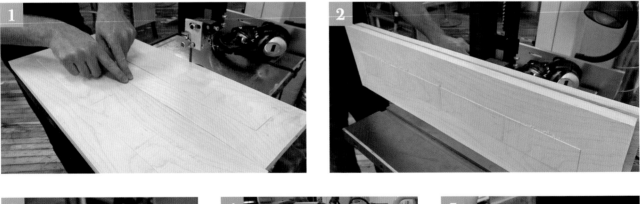

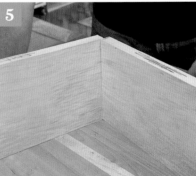

high enough to cut through both the side piece and the clamping block with each pass.

This box is constructed out of four pieces—two long sides and two short sides. First cut one edge of the four pieces, then put a clamping block on your miter fence at the desired length of the short side. Then cut those two short pieces. Next, reset the clamping block to the longer dimension, cutting one right after the others. This ensures perfectly matched pairs (**photo 7**).

Cut the dadoes. Cut the dadoes on the inside faces of all four pieces using a dado blade that's set at $1/4$ in. wide and $3/16$ in. high. Set your rip fence at $1/2$ in. The location of the dadoes should be $1/2$ in. up from the top and bottom edges of the boards. Cut the dadoes in all four pieces, which gives you two cuts on each piece. Next, set the location of the lid by moving the fence. Instead of resetting the dado blades to $1/2$ in., you can make two passes with the $1/4$-in. dado by making a first pass on all four pieces before moving the rip fence another $1/4$ in. and doing a second pass that will create a $1/2$-in.-wide dado. The $1/2$-in. dado marks the point where the box will be cut apart, and it will house the beading that registers the top (**photo 8**).

Cut the miters. Using an L-fence on the tablesaw, cut the miters on the ends of the side pieces (**photo 9**). Set the L-fence so that it's higher than the tip of the blade but still low enough to catch the end of the clamping block. After making a test pass on two pieces, dry-clamp a corner together and check it with a square to make sure you're cutting the miters at a true 45 degrees (**photo 10**). Make any necessary adjustments to the angle of the blade.

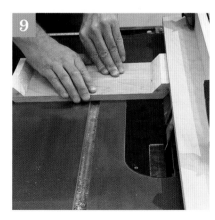

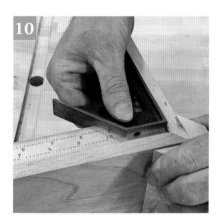

Veneer Details from a Presidential Desk

The inspiration for this project comes from a desk at President John Adams' house in Quincy, Massachusetts, home to four generations of the Adams family.

The desk was made in France and then purchased by Adams and his wife, Abigail, before their return to the United States in 1788. To this day, the desk remains a centerpiece in the president's library (see the top left photo).

The desk is made from a variety of woods, including oak and fruitwood inlays (shown in the top right photo). The detail that served as the inspiration for the lid of the keepsake box is the herringbone pattern made from veneers that were set into a chevron pattern (shown in the bottom photo).

The pattern runs along the entire front of the desk and wraps around the sides as well. It adds a great three-dimensional detail to the piece.

Inside of desk owned by John Adams

Inlays in a variety of woods

Herringbone pattern from veneer

Make the top and bottom.
Assemble the box (without glue), check that the splines fit correctly (see Making Splined Miter Joints on p. 66), and mark the depth of the grooves on the top edges **(photo 11).** Then measure the width and length of the top and bottom directly from these marks and cut the panels to that size. For this project we used $\frac{1}{2}$-in. Baltic birch plywood for the panels. Using a dado blade on the tablesaw, cut a rabbet on all four edges of each panel so the edges fit into the grooves.

T-Mac Tip

Trim the corners of the top and bottom panels so they won't interfere with the splines.

Mark the lid location. Measure the distance from the top edge of a side piece to the top of the $\frac{1}{2}$-in.-wide groove, add $\frac{1}{8}$ in., and mark that dimension on the outside of the box **(photo 12).** This mark will be used to set the tablesaw fence when cutting off the lid later. The object is to center the sawkerf in the slot, so both the lid and the box have a rabbeted edge when cut apart.

Glue up. Dry-fit the entire box one last time, making sure that everything fits properly. Disassemble and then apply a thin and uniform coating of glue to the mitered corners and the grooves for the plywood panels. Add the splines and then assemble and clamp the box together **(photo 13).**

Cut off the blocks. After the glue has set for an hour or so, remove the clamps and cut away most of the clamp blocks on the bandsaw **(photo 14).** Make sure the blade doesn't wander into the box

itself. Remove the balance of the material with a handplane.

Cut the box apart. Set the tablesaw fence so the blade meets the mark you previously made on the outside of the box, then cut the lid away from the box **(photo 15).**

Making Splined Miter Joints

The corners of the box are reinforced with splines that run the full length of the joint. The grain in the splines runs perpendicular to the joint, making it very strong **(photo 1).**

On the tablesaw, move the fence to the right side of the blade, and set the blade at a 45-degree angle. Mark the approximate midway point on the miter **(photo 2).**

To cut the groove, lower the blade until you're sure it will cut less than halfway through the miter, then make a pass over the blade with the clamping block riding firmly against the fence **(photo 3).** Creep up on the final depth until the sawkerf ends at the midway point of the miter.

From a piece of primary material, cut the splines to the correct width and thickness so they fit snugly but can still slide into the kerf **(photo 4).** The exact width is determined by the depth of the sawkerf: Make sure the spline won't prevent the miter from closing up completely when the joint is clamped. If the splines are a little long and protrude from the top of the joint, they can be trimmed back later.

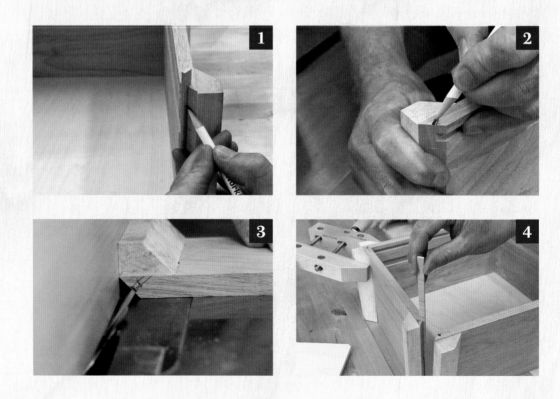

Veneering the lid

The veneered lid is the centerpiece of this project. It's made in several steps from slices of veneer assembled to form a herringbone pattern embellished with triangular and horizontal-grain accents (**photo 1**).

Cut the veneer. From a piece of 12/4 material, cut a blank so the grain runs diagonally to the long edge (**photo 2**). To determine the width of the blank, measure the width of the top and divide by the number of pieces it will take to span the distance evenly. Don't forget to allow for the short-grain pieces that are part of the pattern (see the drawing on p. 60). Rip slices of the blank about 1/16 in. thick on the tablesaw and keep the pieces in sequential order (**photo 3**).

Pair the pieces. Working from the top of the stack, lay down one piece of veneer on the bench, then take the next piece in the stack and fold it over so the two pieces are book-matched and the grain is in a herringbone pattern (**photo 4**).

Shoot the edges. Fold the leaves together, place the pair on a shooting board, and joint the two edges simultaneously with a handplane (**photo 5**).

Tape the pieces together. Open the leaves (face up), align the edges, and tape the two pieces together with veneer tape (**photo 6**).

Set the first pair. Mark the centerline of the lid and glue the first pair of veneer leaves down with yellow glue (or whatever you regularly use) (**photo 7**) so the joint is directly over the centerline.

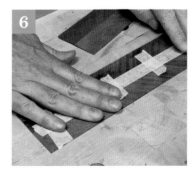

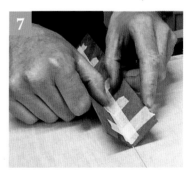

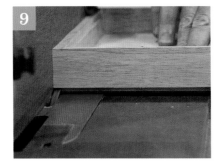

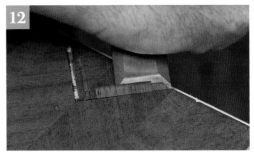

Build the rest of the pattern.
After the glue has set up on the first pair of veneer leaves, continue building the pattern from the center out. Add a strip of horizontal-grain veneer, then another herringbone pair, a horizontal strip, and finally a single strip of diagonally-grained veneer on the outside. Tape each piece in place as you go **(photo 8)**. When the pattern is complete, flip it over as a whole, as if you were opening the page of a book, apply glue, and clamp the veneer to the lid.

T-Mac Tip

Put a piece of waxed paper between the veneer and the caul when clamping the veneer to the lid. The paper will prevent the caul from sticking to the work.

Clean up the edges with a rabbet. After the glue has dried, cut a ¼-in. by ¼-in. rabbet around the perimeter of the lid with a dado blade on the tablesaw **(photo 9)**. Now you can remove all the veneer tape, either with a card scraper, sanding block, or power sander.

Make the triangular accents.
Cut several triangular pieces from the same material you've used for the rest of the veneer **(photo 10)**. On the bandsaw, slice the blocks into a number of pieces slightly thicker than the veneer already on the lid. After each pass, plane the face of the block so it will ride tightly against the fence.

Remove veneer for the triangles. With a combination square and knife, score the veneer on the lid so a triangle will fit into the edge of the pattern, as shown in **photo 11** and in the drawing on p. 60. Continue cutting until the blade goes all the way through the veneer, then carefully remove the veneer with a very sharp chisel. Take care not to pry up along the edges with the chisel, which would splinter the edge **(photo 12)**.

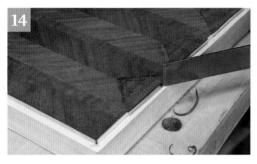

T-Mac Tip

To help the pieces fit together tightly, cut a back bevel in the edge of both sides of each triangle by running it at an angle with the grain using your handplane.

Glue in the triangles. After fitting each triangle, trim to size. Then glue and clamp each triangle into place using a triangular caul and a piece of waxed paper (**photo 13**). Angling the clamp slightly will force the triangle firmly into the slot as the clamp is tightened. To give yourself enough room and allow time for the glue to dry, don't glue the triangles consecutively. Instead, glue in every other one and then come back and fill in the gaps.

Clean up the edges. Once all the triangles have been glued into place and the glue has dried, trim the edges of each triangle, first with a chisel and then with a shoulder plane (**photo 14**) until they are flush with the edge of the rabbet.

Finishing up

Cut the corner beads. Cut ¼-in. by ¼-in. pieces of corner bead. Miter the corners and fit the pieces into the rabbet around the edge of the lid (**photo 1**), then glue and clamp them into place.

Cut the inside bead. On the inside edge of the box, a lip glued into the rabbet helps index the lid when it is closed (**photo 2**). Cut the pieces ³/₁₆ in. by ³/₈ in. and form a roundover profile on the top edge with scratch stock (**photo 3**).

Install the bead on the inside. Cut miters on both ends of the molding, fit them into the rabbet, and then glue them in place one at a time (**photo 4**).

Add the hinges and lips. When the glue on the molding has dried, add the hinges and lips and clean the box with fine sandpaper. You'll then be ready to apply your finish of choice. For this project I used linseed oil, shellac, and wax.

SHAKER NIGHTSTAND

Cutting Traditional Table Joinery and Tapering Legs

This Shaker-inspired nightstand is an excellent introduction to woodworking that teaches fundamentals, such as stock preparation and mortise-and-tenon joinery. The tapered legs and book-matched top are two nice details. Best of all, this table can be made over a long weekend or two, so it will go right from the shop to the bedroom in just a few days.

Although the table could be made from just about any species of wood you have on hand, this one is built with curly maple, a hard, long-wearing wood with a beautiful undulating grain pattern.

Thinking about how grain and color on different parts of the table should relate to each other is a major part of the planning. I oriented the pieces carefully to get the best effect and included a live edge on two of the rails. I also saved a board with an especially interesting grain pattern for the top. The top is glued up from two boards that are mirror images of each other, a technique called book-matching (to learn how to book-match, see Build Your Skills on pp. 80–81).

The haunched mortise-and-tenon joinery is the kind of basic woodworking taught in the first year at my alma mater, the North Bennet Street School in Boston's North End (visit the school in the Road Trip sidebar on p. 74). It's one of the most useful joints you'll learn to make.

Shaker Nightstand

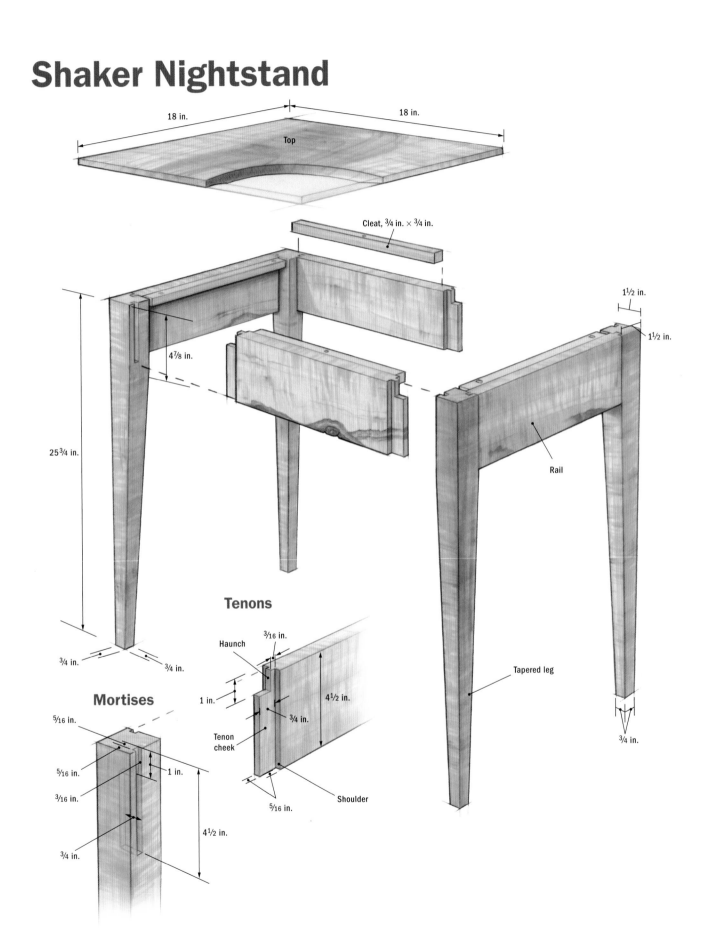

18 in.

18 in.

Top

Cleat, ¾ in. × ¾ in.

1½ in.

1½ in.

4⅞ in.

25¾ in.

Rail

Tenons

¾ in.

¾ in.

Tapered leg

Haunch

3/16 in.

1 in.

4½ in.

¾ in.

Tenon cheek

Shoulder

5/16 in.

¾ in.

Mortises

5/16 in.

5/16 in.

1 in.

3/16 in.

4½ in.

¾ in.

MATERIALS LIST/ROUGH MILL

PART	# OF PIECES	LENGTH (IN.)	WIDTH (IN.)	THICKNESS (IN.)	WOOD	NOTES
Legs	4	26¾	2	1⅝	Primary	
Rails	4	14	5	⅞	Primary	
Top	1	19	18½	⅞	Primary	
Cleats	4	12	1¼	⅞	Secondary	
Screws	6					#8 × 1¼ in.

Rough dimensions are slightly longer, wider and thicker than finished dimensions. Mill the stock, sticker it overnight, and then bring pieces to the finished dimensions the following day.

TOOL LIST

POWER TOOLS
Bandsaw
Circular saw
Cordless drill
Drill press
Jointer
Mortiser
Planer
Tablesaw with
   dado blade

HAND TOOLS
Chisels
Clamps
Combination
   square
Dovetail saw
Handplane
Marking gauge

Laying out the pieces

This table is all about the wood. The parts are simple: four legs and four rails, connected with mortise-and-tenon joinery, and the two-board top.

Position the pieces carefully. With highly figured wood like this hard maple, it's worth spending some time identifying areas you want to highlight in the finished piece. Before cutting up the plank, I found a section of grain I wanted to save for the top (**photo 1**). Less figured material toward the edge of the plank would be a good choice for the legs (**photo 2**).

Mill the parts. Lay out the parts for the table on the face of the plank and cut them to rough size with a circular saw (1 in. greater in length, ½ in. greater in width, and ⅛ in. to ³/₁₆ in. greater in thickness). Flatten one face and joint one edge, use a thickness planer to make the second face parallel to the first, and, finally, use the tablesaw to make the second edge parallel to the first. Then sticker the parts overnight. In the morning, you may notice that some of the parts aren't as straight as they were the

day before (**photo 3**). Remill the pieces to their finished dimensions and remove all mill marks with a handplane.

Visiting the Nation's Oldest Trade School

I learned woodworking at the North Bennet Street School, the oldest trade school in the United States. The school was founded in 1881 as a place where recent immigrants living in Boston's North End could get a variety of social services, including English lessons and training in woodworking.

In 1985, the school turned to crafts training for adults and currently runs seven other programs in addition to furniture making.

In the school's gallery, you'll see some of the students' outstanding work, such as the curly maple chest shown in the top left photo below, which is embellished inside and out with ebony, and the Federal-style sideboard with tambour doors and carved grape details on the legs in the bottom left photo below.

In the upper bench room, students take on projects required for graduation: a chair, table, and case piece. With its compound-angle joinery, the chair is a real challenge to build.

Downstairs, in a part of the school called "the incubator," students learn basic woodworking skills, like how to make a mortise-and-tenon joint. Getting the fundamentals right prepares students to tackle complex projects as they move through the program.

Work of the students at North Bennet Street School (above and right)

Making a mortise-and-tenon joint, a basic skill taught at North Bennet Street

Making the legs

Before doing any joinery on the legs, choose the faces you want to be most prominent in your project. For example, I chose a dark piece for one of the legs that would be at the front of the table when it was finished (**photo 1**).

Label the tops of the legs. Once you've examined the pieces and made your decisions, label the tops of the legs so you won't get them mixed up when cutting the mortises and the tapers (**photo 2**).

Lay out the mortises. The haunched mortise (**photo 3**) helps stabilize the joint and keep the pieces straight. To help visualize how the joinery will go together, use a combination square to lay out the locations of the mortises on the tops of the legs. These mortises will be $5/16$ in. wide, so I'll leave an equal amount of material on the outside of the leg (**photo 4**). The tenons will be $3/4$ in. long, short enough so they don't run into each other inside the leg. I can get that dimension directly from the layout marks made on the top of the leg. I also lay out the depth of the haunch, roughly $3/16$ in., and length, $15/16$ in., and mark the length of the mortise (**photo 5**) on the leg. After marking one leg, it can be used as a template to mark the layout lines on the other legs.

Mark the edges of the mortises. With a marking gauge, scribe a line representing the outside edges of the mortises (**photo 6**).

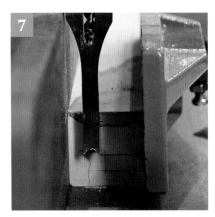

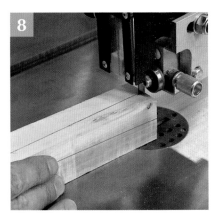

T-Mac Tip

Leave a little material between each hole you make with the mortiser, then go back and clean up these webs. This will help keep the chisel from flexing and ensure the holes stay straight.

Cut the mortises. Use a mortising machine to cut the mortises, or if you don't have one, use a drill press or a drill and chisels. Before plunging into the wood, make sure the mortise chisel is square to the fence and set to the right depth (**photo 7**). Remember that the haunch and the mortise are cut to different depths. You can eyeball the depth of the haunch by plunging the mortise chisel to $^1/8$ in. to $^3/16$ in. deep. After the mortising machine has done its work, clean up the mortises and the haunches with bench chisels.

Lay out and cut the tapers. Each leg is tapered on its two inside faces, beginning about $^1/4$ in. below the end of the mortise and running all the way to the bottom of the leg. The bottoms of the legs are $^3/4$ in. square. Use a straightedge to draw lines on the inside faces of the legs that connect the start and stop points of each taper.

Cut the tapers. Although several tools would do this job, I cut the tapers on the bandsaw (**photo 8**). Make one cut along a layout line, then tape the offcut back to the leg to restore the layout line you've just cut away and make the second cut (**photo 9**). Then remove the mill marks from the legs with a handplane.

Making the tenons

You'll need to cut a tenon on each end of all the rails. The outside of the rail is flush with the outer face of the leg, which means the cheek cuts on the inside and outside faces of the rail pieces will be different.

Mark the outside face of the tenon. With the marking gauge still set to $5/16$ in. (from laying out the mortises), scribe a line on the end of each rail piece. Use the outer face of the rail as your reference face (**photo 1**).

Mark the shoulder lines. With another marking gauge (or after resetting the first one), mark the shoulder lines on the rails. These lines represent the length of the tenons, in this case $3/4$ in. (**photo 2**).

Mark the inside face of the tenon. Reset the marking gauge, using the inside of the mortise as a guide, and strike a second line on the ends of the rails (**photo 3**). Once again, index the gauge from the outside face of the rails. These lines represent the back edge of the tenon.

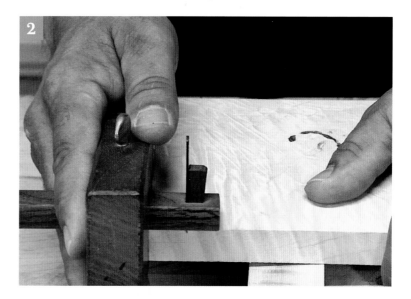

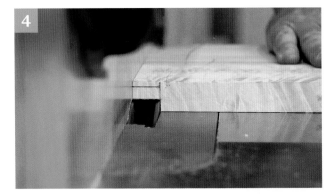

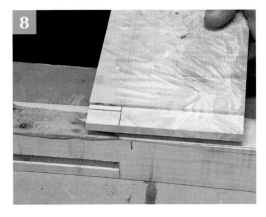

Cut the outside face of the tenons. Set up a $7/8$-in. dado set on the tablesaw and bury $1/8$ in. of the stack in a sacrificial wood fence. Then adjust the fence and blade height so the dado will cut to the shoulder line and just a hair beneath the cheek line (**photo 4**). Using a backer block with the saw provides some support and stability when making cuts. Check to make sure that the outside face of the rails is flush with the outside face of the leg (**photo 5**). Cut all the outside cheeks at this setting.

Cut the inside face of the tenons. Readjust the blade height to cut the inside cheeks of the tenons to the scribed lines (**photo 6**).

Fine-tune the fit. Use a shoulder plane to shave the inside cheek of the tenons so they fit snugly in the mortises

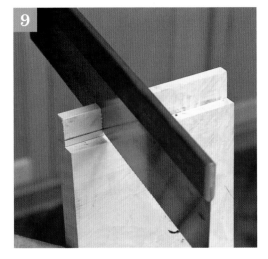

(**photo 7**). Be careful not to remove too much material.

Lay out the haunch. Use a combination square to mark the depth and length of the haunch on the tenon (**photo 8**), and then cut the haunch with a dovetail saw (**photo 9**).

Dry-fitting and assembly

Dry-fit the table. When all of the pieces have been cut and fitted, it's time to assemble all of the parts in a dry-fit—that is, without glue. This is the time to make any necessary adjustments. You can check the table for square by measuring the diagonals between the inside corners of the legs. When the measurements are the same, the table is square **(photo 1)**.

If the table isn't square, double-check that the rail pieces are all the right length and that the mortised edges of the legs are square to each other. Skewing the clamps slightly also can bring an out-of-square assembly back into alignment.

Glue up the pieces. Now the table can be taken apart, glue applied to the mortises and tenons, and the parts clamped together again.

Add cleats for the top. To attach the top, add cleats with predrilled holes to the inside edges of the rails **(photo 2)**. After the top has been glued together, planed, and sanded, screw it in place through the cleats (for more on gluing up the book-matched top, see Build Your Skills on pp. 80-81).

Book-Matching a Tabletop

Book-matching means to slice open a piece of wood along its length and unfold it, just like the pages of a book, to create two pieces that are mirror images of each other.

This technique is a great way to emphasize dramatic grain patterns. If the most interesting grain is located near one edge of the piece, the pattern will be near the center of the top after it's been book-matched.

Start with a piece of stock more than twice as thick as the finished top. I made the top on this nightstand from rough material that's 2½ in. thick.

Make a cut on each edge midway through the board **(photo 1)**. Make several passes, raising the tablesaw blade each time until the blade has reached its maximum height.

Finish the cut on the bandsaw. With a board this thick, and with the two relief cuts made by the tablesaw, the blank can be cut safely without a fence **(photo 2)**. Then take the pieces through the finish mill process so they are flat and smooth **(photo 3)**.

Fold the two pieces together face to face, put them in a vise, and shoot the two edges simultaneously with a handplane

(photo 4). This ensures the edges will line up correctly—even if the angle of the plane isn't exactly square to the edge. Make an extra pass near the center of the board to make a spring joint, which will keep the ends of the butt joint very tight.

Apply yellow glue to the edges and a clamp across the joint at the center. Then add a clamp at each end. After the glue has dried, cut a bevel on the bottom edge of the top all the way around to make it look lighter **(photo 5).** The outside edge on this top is ⅝ in. thick.

Finish the table with your finish of choice. I used my favorite combination: boiled linseed oil, shellac, and wax (for more finishing, see pp. 162–181).

FLAG BOX

Cutting Splines for Miter Joints

A flag box is an attractive way to display and protect a folded American flag, and it makes a special gift for a military veteran or the family of a veteran. This is a small project, but it has some complicated parts, making it a challenging but doable project.

This flag box is made from red oak, a traditional American hardwood that is both durable and abundant. The three-sided box is joined at the corners with miters that have been reinforced with hardwood splines, in this case live oak that was originally part of the USS *Constitution* (see my Road Trip to Old Ironsides on p. 88).

The miters at one corner are cut at 45 degrees, but those on the other two corners are half of that, $22^1/_2$ degrees. These very steep miters are cut with the help of an easy-to-make jig that holds the material vertically against a tablesaw fence. Splines reinforce the miters and add a decorative touch (see Build Your Skills on pp. 92–93).

The back of the box is a piece of plywood let into rabbets cut in the sides of the box. On the front, I used a sheet of nonglare glass.

Finally, there is the matter of folding the flag. We were honored to have the help of several hometown heroes, veterans from Canton, Massachusetts, who demonstrated the proper technique in a heart-felt ceremony (the sidebar on p. 94 shows how).

Flag Box

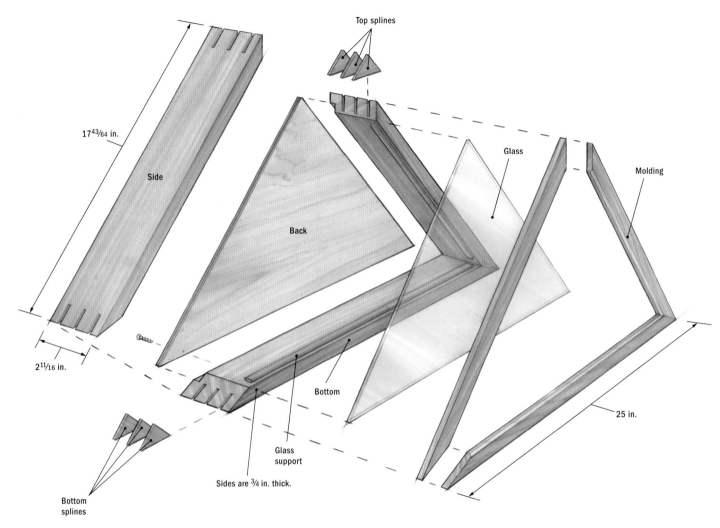

Top splines

17⁴³⁄₆₄ in.

Side

2¹¹⁄₁₆ in.

Back

Glass

Molding

Bottom

Glass
support

Sides are ¾ in. thick.

Bottom
splines

25 in.

Rabbet

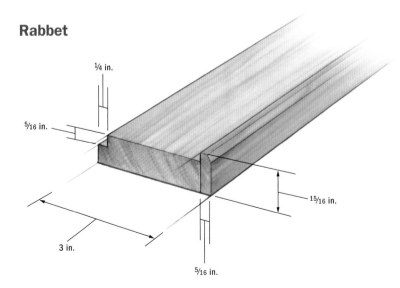

¼ in.

⁵⁄₁₆ in.

3 in.

⁵⁄₁₆ in.

¹⁵⁄₁₆ in.

MATERIALS LIST/ROUGH MILL

PART	# OF PIECES	LENGTH (IN.)	WIDTH (IN.)	THICKNESS (IN.)	WOOD	NOTES
Bottom	1	26	3³⁄₁₆	⁷⁄₈	Primary	
Sides	2	18⁴³⁄₆₄	3³⁄₁₆	⁷⁄₈	Primary	
Bottom molding	1	26	1½	⁷⁄₁₆	Primary	
Side molding	2	18⁴³⁄₆₄	1½	⁷⁄₁₆	Primary	
Top splines	3	2¹⁹⁄₃₂	1³⁄₈	¼	Hardwood	
Bottom splines	6	2³⁄₆₄	1³⁄₈	¼	Hardwood	
Glass supports	3	16	³⁄₁₆	⁵⁄₁₆	Secondary	
Glass	1					⅛ in. thick, fit to case
Brads	9					⅜ in. long
Screws	6					#6 × ½ in.
Plywood	1					2 ft. × 1 ft. × ¼ in. for back
Plywood	1					4 ft. × 4 ft. × ¾ in. for jigs

Rough dimensions are slightly longer, wider and thicker than finished dimensions. Mill the stock, sticker it overnight, and then bring pieces to the finished dimensions the following day.

TOOL LIST

POWER TOOLS
Bandsaw
Cordless drill
Jointer
Planer
Router
Tablesaw

HAND TOOLS
Card scraper
Clamps
Hammer
Handplane
Handsaw
Mill file

Making the box sides

The sides of the box are ³⁄₄ in. thick and 2¹¹⁄₁₆ in. wide. The pieces are laid out with chalk on the face of a plank, making them slightly larger than their finished dimensions.

Rough mill the pieces. Once the pieces for the sides and the edge molding have been cut from the plank, rough mill them with a jointer and thickness planer and sticker them overnight (**photo 1**). The next day, they can be cut to their final dimensions and planed with a no. 4½ plane to remove the mill marks. The pieces are now ready for joinery.

Cut the rabbets. The bottom inside edge of each side piece gets a ¼-in. by 5/16-in. rabbet to accept the plywood bottom (**photo 2**). It can be cut on a tablesaw or with a handplane, or, as I did here, on a router table with a rabbeting bit. The width of the rabbet is determined by the diameter of the bearing on the end of the bit. This one will cut a rabbet ¼ in. wide (**photo 3**). Adjust the height of the router so the depth of cut will be 5/16 in. An important feature of this router table is the pivoting pin, which allows the stock to be tipped safely into the turning bit (**photo 4**). Once the cutterhead has been set, move the fence so the guard is over the bit (**photo 5**). Note: Be sure to use eye and hearing protection while cutting the rabbets on all three pieces.

Add the molding. The top edges of the sides get a strip of molding 5/16 in. thick by 13/16 in. wide that forms a lip for the glass. Start by cutting strips from the side pieces you have already rough-milled

(**photo 6**). Remove the mill marks with a handplane, then glue each strip on the top edge of each side piece (**photo 7**).

T-Mac Tip

Glue squeeze-out would interfere with the fit of the glass. Mark the molding strip with pencil so you know not to apply glue on the portion  of the molding that will be inside the case where the glass will rest.

Clean up the edge. After the glue has dried, the molding might be slightly proud on the face (**photo 8**). If that's the case, use a handplane to flush up the face of each piece and remove any glue residue (**photo 9**). Next, parallel the two edges on all three pieces at the tablesaw with the same tablesaw setting. This will ensure that all the pieces are exactly the same width (**photo 10**). Finally, tilt the blade to 45 degrees and cut a decorative chamfer on the inside edge of the strip.

A Piece of Old Ironsides

The USS *Constitution*

Copper fasteners on the ship

The USS *Constitution* got its nickname "Old Ironsides" during a battle in the War of 1812, 300 miles off the coast of Nova Scotia. As British cannonballs bounced off the ship's thick oak hull, an American sailor cried out "she must be made of iron."

The ship is actually built of several types of wood, including live and white oak. It's now undergoing a restoration at its berth at the former Charlestown Navy Yard in Boston, shown in the top left photo.

Launched in 1797, the ship is the world's oldest commissioned naval vessel afloat. Deep in the hold, you can still see original parts of the ship that are more than 200 years old, including copper fasteners supplied by Paul Revere (see the bottom photo at left).

In the USS *Constitution*'s repair shop, work is under way to make replacement cap rails out of white oak (shown in the left photo below). The laminated rails are 35 ft. long, 7 in. thick, and as much as 25 in. wide and will be placed on the ship with the help of a crane.

After touring the ship and the shop, I was given a piece of live oak that was removed during the restoration (see the photo below). I felt privileged to use this wood for the splines in our flag box.

Live oak from the USS *Constitution* for the flag box

White oak for the restoration

Cutting the miters

Make the jig. The $22\frac{1}{2}$-degree miters on the ends of the long side pieces look difficult to cut, but a tablesaw jig makes the process extremely simple. The jig is made by screwing several pieces of scrap plywood together and will provide support to the side pieces while making the cuts. Note: Be sure that the upright backer block is at right angles to the table (**photo 1**).

Mark the orientation of the pieces. To avoid cutting the miters in the wrong direction, orient the pieces in their proper locations and mark the inside face of each piece to indicate which edges will be cut at a 45-degree angle and which will be cut at $22\frac{1}{2}$ degrees (**photo 2**).

Cut the $22\frac{1}{2}$-degree miters. Both ends of the long piece are cut at $22\frac{1}{2}$ degrees; one end of each of the short pieces also gets a miter at this angle. Make sure you are cutting the correct ends of the short pieces—there should be one left and one right. Before cutting the miters, set your saw to what you think is $22\frac{1}{2}$ degrees. Cut a couple of scrap pieces in the upright position using the jig, and then put the pieces together. Check to see that the two pieces together form a 45-degree angle. This may take some finessing and it's the most challenging part of the project. Once you're ready to cut, clamp the workpiece to the jig (again in the upright position) and run the workpiece over the blade (**photo 3**).

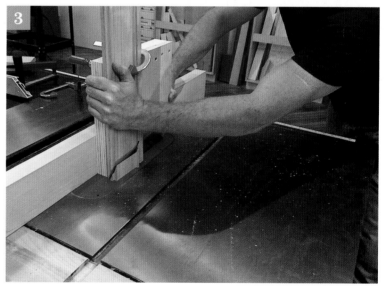

Save the offcuts—they will come in handy during glue-up (**photo 4**).

Cut the 45-degree miters. Now cut the two 45-degree miters for the square corner of the box. You'll need a spacer block to go beneath the workpiece so it lays dead flat on the tablesaw (**photo 5**). Cut the two miters so the pieces are slightly long; creep up on the fit by testing the corners of the box. When the miter is still open on the inside, it means that a little more material can be shaved from the miter to make it fit (**photo 6**).

T-Mac Tip

To prevent tearout on the face of the box, place a piece of scrap between the side piece and the backer block on the jig before running the piece over the tablesaw.

Gluing up the box

After all the miters fit correctly, it's time to glue up the box. Ordinarily, clamping the corners would be a challenge—you could use a few pins or spring clamps to keep the corners tight, but both of those approaches have their drawbacks. To simplify the process, use the saved offcut pieces from the miters as clamping blocks.

Glue on the clamping blocks. Working one at a time, apply a small amount of glue to the back of each block and attach the block to the corresponding angle by rubbing it back and forth until it starts to grab. Be sure and keep each block away from the very edge of the workpiece (**photo 1**). Glue blocks on each outside face of all three side pieces at the corners.

Apply the clamps. Let the glue dry for a half-hour or so, then glue and clamp the corners together. Although it's possible to use C-clamps here, hand screws are better because they apply pressure along the full width of the joint (**photo 2**).

Remove the blocks. After the glue has dried for a couple of hours, the clamps can be removed (**photo 3**) and the blocks cut away. Using a bandsaw or handsaw, cut off the blocks. Be careful not to cut into the sides of the project. Any remaining block material can be removed at the bench using a handplane, card scraper, or electrical sander. Work until the surfaces are flat and clean (**photo 4**).

Adding Splines to a Miter Joint

Adding splines to a miter joint makes the joint much stronger, and using a contrasting wood adds an interesting visual detail.

Mark the box where you want to insert the splines. Locate one at the center of each corner, then divide the remaining spaces in half, for a total of three splines at each corner **(photo 1)**.

Make a jig from pieces of scrap plywood to form a 90-degree angle in which the box will sit **(photo 2).** This will provide proper support and safety while the box passes over the tablesaw blade.

Before making the cuts, mark a line diagonally across the corner by measuring out an equal distance on each side piece (here, that's 1¼ in.) and connect the dots. Set the blade height to the line, making sure the cut will not break through the inside of the box **(photo 3).** Then set the fence so the blade lines up with the spline marks on the box, clamp the box to the jig, and make the cuts. When making the cuts

on the very sharp corners, add some 22½-degree blocks to the jig and adjust the height of the blade so the splines will be of even length all the way around the box **(photo 4).**

Cut off some strips of wood for the splines slightly thicker than the width of the sawkerf and plane them until the splines fit snugly in the kerfs. Use a mill file to flatten the bottom of all nine slots **(photo 5).** Mark out the number of splines you'll need from the strips and cut out the pieces **(photo 6).** Add glue and fit the splines. After the glue has dried, plane away the excess.

Folding the Flag

Veterans from the Canton, Massachusetts, Veterans Honor Guard came to the shop to show how a flag is folded correctly.

The flag is held at the corners, then folded lengthwise twice, the second time so that the stars and blue background are on the outside, as shown in Step 1.

Then, beginning at the end opposite the stars, the flag is folded into a triangular shape (Step 2), with the top edges tightly aligned. The first fold symbolizes life. The second fold symbolizes the belief in eternal life. The third fold is in honor of veterans who have served.

The flag continues to be folded, maintaining the triangular shape up toward the stars and blue background (see Step 3). When the flag is completely folded, with the stars showing, the final edge is tucked inside (Step 4).

Legend has it that once the flag has been folded it should never be unfolded because it contains the spirit of a fallen warrior.

Folding the flag, step 1

Folding the flag, step 2

Folding the flag, step 3

Folding the flag, step 4

Honoring the flag and U.S. veterans

Finishing up

The only things left to do are to cut out and attach the plywood back and to make the glass front.

Lay out the back. Place the box on a sheet of 1/4-in. shop-grade plywood and trace the outside perimeter. Then subtract 3/8 in. for the rabbet and draw a second set of lines inside the first **(photo 1)**. Cut the piece and make any adjustments so it fits inside the rabbet **(photo 2)**.

Finish the case. Before the glass and the flag can be added, you need to apply finish to the box. This one is finished with three coats of catalyzed lacquer, which dries very quickly, but you can use the finish of your choice.

Fit the glass. The glass fits inside the box and is held in place by the top molding strips on the outside. To secure the glass from the inside, cut strips of wood about 3/16 in. by 1/2 in. Predrill small holes (big enough for a brad), carefully position the glass from the inside, and then tap in the brads **(photo 3)**. You are now ready to add the flag (see Folding the Flag on the facing page).

Screw in the back. After the flag is safely inside the box, attach the plywood back with wood screws.

SERVING TRAY

Mastering Compound Angles

If you've been frustrated by compound miters, this serving tray is a great way to put that behind you. The focus here is on simplicity, starting with the design. Given one trick, the compound miters that allow the top to flare outward are actually simple to make.

Like many furniture makers, I used to make compound angles fit through trial and error, wasting a lot of material in the process. Then I was shown how to make a "magic" block, a gauge block that's used on the tablesaw to set both the blade and miter-gauge angles for joints that fit together perfectly. There's no math involved.

Compound joinery is key to some very complex furniture forms, including a Boston bombé secretary I made a few years ago. This distinctive style dates from 18th-century New England, showing up not only in case furniture but even in an early church pulpit (see my Road Trip to The First Church in Ipswich, Massachusetts, on p. 102).

All of the joinery is cut on the tablesaw, and the sides and bottom are put together with old-fashioned cut nails. Even the finish is simple and quick. Although I often use an oil–shellac–wax finish on my projects, this time I chose to finish the tray with only wax. It's easy to apply and it allows the color to be fine-tuned (see Build Your Skills on p. 104). It also sets off the beautiful figure in the quartersawn white oak that this tray was made from.

Serving Tray

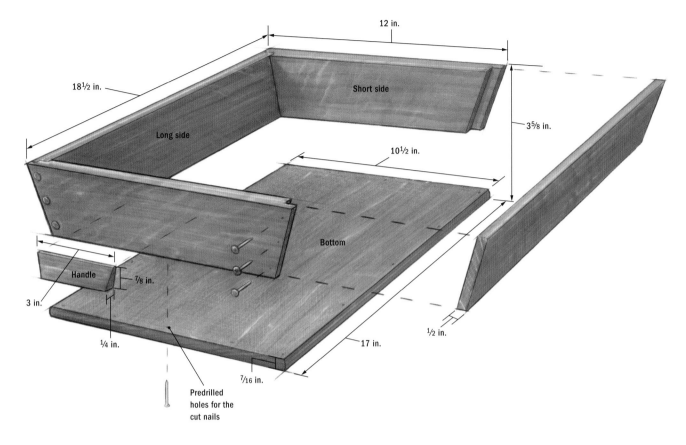

12 in.

18¹⁄₂ in.

Short side

Long side

3⁵⁄₈ in.

10¹⁄₂ in.

Bottom

Handle

⁷⁄₈ in.

3 in.

¹⁄₄ in.

17 in.

¹⁄₂ in.

⁷⁄₁₆ in.

Predrilled
holes for the
cut nails

Rabbets

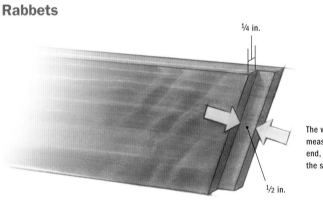

¹⁄₄ in.

The width of the rabbet is
measured perpendicular to the
end, just like the thickness of
the sides.

¹⁄₂ in.

MATERIALS LIST/ROUGH MILL

PART	# OF PIECES	LENGTH (IN.)	WIDTH (IN.)	THICKNESS (IN.)	WOOD	NOTES
Short Sides	2	13	4	$5/8$	Primary	
Long sides	2	19	4	$5/8$	Primary	
Bottom	1	18	11	$9/16$	Primary	
Handles	2	4	2	2	Primary	
Wrought nails	12					1 in. long
Cut nails	14					1 in. long

Rough dimensions are slightly longer, wider and thicker than finished dimensions. Mill the stock, sticker it overnight, and then bring pieces to the finished dimensions the following day.

POWER TOOLS
Circular saw
Drill
Jointer
Planer
Tablesaw

HAND TOOLS
Bevel gauge
Clamps
Hammer
Handplane
Marking gauge
Miter gauge

Getting started

All of the joinery for the tray stems from a gauge block, which is made by crosscutting its two ends and ripping one edge at the desired angle on the tablesaw. The only measurement you'll need is the angle you choose for the slope of all four sides. After that, it's just a question of setting the tablesaw blade and miter-gauge angles to the block.

Rough-mill the parts. Start by laying out the pieces for the tray on the rough stock. Mark the pieces so that the grain will run in the same direction all the way around the finished tray (**photo 1**). After rough-milling the pieces, allow them to acclimate overnight and bring them to their finished dimensions the following day. Note: Keep the rough width dimension even during finish milling.

Lay out and mark the pieces. Lay out the pieces on the bench as you want them oriented in the tray, and mark the bottom of the inside faces (**photo 2**). Also mark the left and the right end of each piece. This helps keep the

pieces oriented correctly as the edges and ends are cut on the tablesaw.

Set the bevel angle. Choose an angle for the sides and set a bevel gauge to that angle. The sides of this tray slope

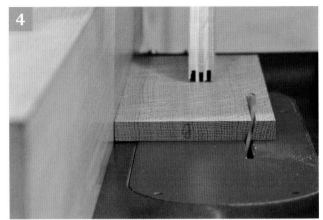

outward at 72 degrees. Transfer that angle to the tablesaw blade (photo 3).

Rip to width. Orient a piece against the fence so the long point of the angle will be on the inside of the bottom edge or the outside of the top edge. Rip one edge (photo 4), flip the board over, and, without changing the position of the fence, rip the second edge so the tray side is at its finished width (photo 5). Repeat the process on the remaining three pieces.

Make the "magic" block. Select a piece of 2-in.-thick scrap and without changing the setting of the tablesaw blade, crosscut each end (photo 6) and then rip one edge to the same angle (photo 7).

Reset the blade angle. With the ripped edge of the block face down on the tablesaw, adjust the blade until it matches the angle in the end of the block (photo 8). The block will not be perpendicular to the blade.

Set the miter gauge. With the end of the block tight against the blade, adjust the miter gauge so it's at the same angle as the edge of the block (photo 9).

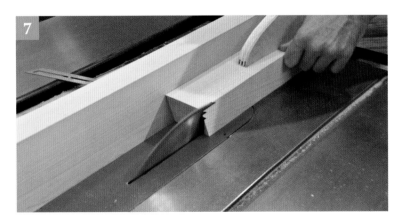

Cut the first end. Using the miter gauge, cut one end of all the sides pieces. Be certain you're cutting the correct end: In this case, the right side of each piece is being crosscut (**photo 10**). A block clamped to the miter gauge will ensure the workpiece doesn't move.

Move the miter gauge. Move the miter gauge to the slot on the other side of the blade, and reposition and screw the fence on the miter gauge so it's out of the way of the blade. Do not change the angle of the blade or the angle of the miter gauge (**photo 11**).

Cut the left side. Take one of the side pieces you have just cut, flip it over so the face that was down on the tablesaw is now facing up, and position it against the miter gauge (**photo 12**). Mark the finished length of the piece on the edge, and clamp a block to the miter gauge fence to keep the piece in place. Then make the cut.

T-Mac Tip

Cut similar pieces without changing the position of the block on the miter gauge fence to ensure that the ends and sides will be exactly the same length. That is, cut both long side pieces, then cut both short end pieces.

Lessons from an 18th-Century Pulpit

The historical roots for the tray's flared shape can be found in a 250-year-old pulpit made in the bombé style that now resides at The First Church in Ipswich, Massachusetts.

Built in 1749, the pulpit came from the fourth church built on the hilltop property. It was later moved to yet another church on the site and rescued when that building burned in 1965. It's now safely ensconced in the modern church that took its place.

The pulpit shown in the photos below left and at right is an exceptionally important example of early New England woodworking. It has the characteristic kettle base of bombé furniture and is still in excellent condition. Made by a local cabinetmaker named Abraham Knowlton, it predates the earliest known example of bombé furniture.

When I made my serpentine-front Boston bombé secretary, the drawer sides had to be joined with compound miters so they would fit the curves of the chest base (shown in the bottom photo below). The basic approach was the same as it is with this serving tray.

Pulpit features kettle base of bombé furniture

Inspiration from a 250-year-old pulpit

Serpentine drawer front

Cutting the rabbets

Mark the ends. With a marking gauge set to the thickness of the stock, scribe a line on the inside face at each end of the short side pieces (**photo 1**).

Set the depth. Reset the marking gauge for half the thickness of the stock and mark the ends of the short side pieces (**photo 2**).

Cut the rabbets. Lower the tablesaw blade so it meets the reference line on the end of a short side piece (about ¼ in. high) and adjust the fence so the blade will meet the reference line on the face of the piece. Do not change the angle of the blade. Now make a series of passes over the blade to cut the rabbet. Do the same thing on the other short end piece (**photo 3**).

Cut the other side. Flip the side piece end for end, readjust the miter gauge fence so it matches the angle on the workpiece, and cut the rabbet on the other end of both side pieces (**photo 4**). Clean up the rabbets with a router plane or a shoulder plane to eliminate the saw marks.

Applying a Wax Finish

I often use an oil–shellac–wax finish on my projects, but for the serving tray I've chosen something a little simpler: wax. It's easy to apply and forgiving of mistakes, and different-colored waxes can be applied in layers to subtly change the color of the wood.

Using 150-grit sandpaper, sand all surfaces of the tray and break any sharp edges.

Dip a clean, lint-free rag into the wax and wipe it on **(photo 1).** You can apply it in a straight or circular motion and even go cross-grain—it doesn't matter. Be sure to work the wax into the corners. Adjust the color by applying another coat of wax in a different color **(photo 2).** You don't have to wait for the first coat to dry before applying another one.

Once the wax is dry, buff it out with a clean, soft cloth **(photo 3).**

T-Mac Tip

Experiment with different waxes on a sample board before applying any to your project. How many coats you apply is really a matter of personal taste.

Assembling the tray

Make angled cauls. Make a pair of angled cauls by gluing blocks cut to the same angle as the sides of the tray to scraps of ¼-in. plywood (**photo 1**). Hold the sides of the tray together initially with tape, then use the cauls to clamp the pieces together.

Drill for nails. Mark nail locations on the ends and drill pilot holes (**photo 2**).

Glue up the tray. Remove the clamps, apply glue to the rabbets, and reassemble the tray with clamps. To keep the corners aligned, clamp the tray to the bench with cauls that span the tray's width (**photo 3**). Now nail the corners together with the wrought nails (**photo 4**). When the clamps are removed, any misalignment of the top edges can be flushed up with a plane or a sander.

Add the bottom and handles. Glue up a blank of sufficient width to overhang the sides of the tray by about ¼ in. and round over the edges with a plane. Nail the bottom on with cut nails after drilling pilot holes (**photo 5**). Rip thin pieces of material at the same angle as the sides and glue them onto the ends of the tray for handles (**photo 6**).

Finish the tray. Apply a wax finish, following the directions in Applying a Wax Finish on the facing page.

BREAD BOX

TECHNIQUE

Making a Tambour Door

This bread box is a great project that will add a nice accent to any kitchen, and while small, it is surprisingly challenging to build. Its main feature is a tambour door that slides in a groove and, when opened, is concealed behind a false back inside the box.

The tambour door is made from a number of individual slats glued to a canvas backing. Construction is simplified by the use of a well-designed jig (see Build Your Skills on pp. 116–119). Although a breadbox isn't overly complex, the inspiration for the door comes from two rare pieces of early American furniture housed at the Peabody Essex Museum (which I visited in the Road Trip on p. 112).

Half-blind dovetails join parts of the box together. This is a good project for practicing these joints because most of the dovetails are on the bottom of the box, where they will never show. Start there, and by the time you make the dovetailed top piece you'll be warmed up.

The rounded sides of the box are made with a template and router. There's also some work to do on both a router table and a tablesaw, but the techniques are straightforward. This project doesn't require a great amount of material, and it can even be built with wood you have hanging around the shop. In this case we opted for some choice cherry.

Bread Box

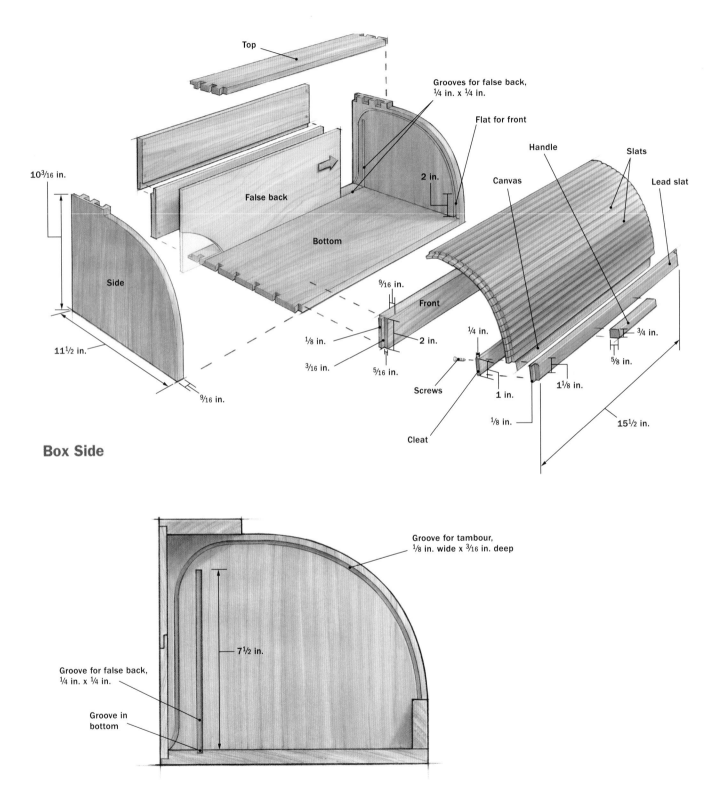

Top

Grooves for false back,
¼ in. x ¼ in.

Flat for front

Handle

Slats

Canvas

Lead slat

2 in.

False back

10³⁄₁₆ in.

Side

Bottom

9⁄₁₆ in.

Front

11½ in.

1⁄₈ in.

3⁄₁₆ in.

5⁄₁₆ in.

2 in.

¼ in.

¾ in.

5⁄₈ in.

9⁄₁₆ in.

Screws

1 in.

1⁄₈ in.

1¹⁄₈ in.

15½ in.

Cleat

Box Side

Groove for tambour,
1⁄₈ in. wide x 3⁄₁₆ in. deep

7½ in.

Groove for false back,
¼ in. x ¼ in.

Groove in
bottom

MATERIALS LIST/ROUGH MILL

PART	# OF PIECES	LENGTH (IN.)	WIDTH (IN.)	THICKNESS (IN.)	WOOD	NOTES
Sides	2	$11^3/_{16}$	12	$^{11}/_{16}$	Primary	
Bottom	1	$16^7/_8$	12	$^{11}/_{16}$	Primary	
Top	1	$16^7/_8$	4	$^{11}/_{16}$	Primary	
Front	1	$16^1/_2$	$2^1/_2$	$^{11}/_{16}$	Primary	
Shiplap back	2	$16^7/_8$	$5^1/_2$	$^1/_2$	Primary	
Slats	3	$16^1/_2$	5	$^9/_{16}$	Primary	
Lead slat	1	$16^1/_2$	$1^5/_8$	$^9/_{16}$	Primary	
Handle	1	$7^1/_2$	$1^1/_4$	$^3/_4$	Primary	
Cleat	1	$15^1/_2$	$1^1/_2$	$^3/_8$	Primary	
Canvas						$^1/_2$ yd., 8-oz., unprimed cotton artist's canvas
Screws	8					#8 × 1 in. for jig
Screws	12					#4 or #6 × $^1/_2$ in. for shiplap and lead slat/cleat
$^1/_4$-in. plywood	1					$15^5/_8$ in. × $7^5/_8$ in. for false back
$^3/_4$-in. plywood	1					18 in. × 20 in. for tambour jig
$^3/_4$-in. MDF						$11^1/_2$ in. × $10^3/_{16}$ in. for template

Rough dimensions are slightly longer, wider and thicker than finished dimensions. Mill the stock, sticker it overnight, and then bring pieces to the finished dimensions the following day.

TOOL LIST

POWER TOOLS

Bandsaw
Circular saw
Drill
Jointer
Planer
Router
Router table
Tablesaw with
  dado blade

HAND TOOLS

Chisels
Clamps
Combination
  square
Compass
Dovetail saw
File
Handplane
Mallet
Marking gauge
Putty knife
Rasp
Sander

Making the box

Lay out the pieces. Lay out the sides, back, bottom, top, and a blank for the tambour slats on the rough material. Take care to stay away from defects in the wood, and choose straight-grained areas for the sides and especially for the tambours **(photo 1)**. Rough-mill the stock, allow it to acclimate overnight, and then finish-mill the pieces the following day.

Scribe the dovetail baselines. To mark the baselines for the pins, use a marking gauge set to the thickness of the stock and scribe a line on the top and bottom inside faces of the side pieces **(photo 2)**.

Reset the marking gauge to $^3/_8$ in. (or use a second marking gauge) and scribe lines on both sides and both edges of the top and bottom pieces. These are the baselines for the tails. With the marking gauge at the same setting, scribe a line on the top and bottom edge of the side pieces, with the fence of the gauge running on the inside face of the stock **(photo 3)**.

T-Mac Tip

For some of us, creating a beautiful dovetail is as good as it gets. It challenges our ability to create something with precision and accuracy. On this piece, the top dovetails are visible and, as a result, worth the effort. The dovetails on the bottom of the box, however, are purely functional. There is less need to agonize over getting them just right.

Lay out the pins. Mark the pins on the bottom edge of the side pieces, making the pin centers no more than 2 in. apart. Don't worry too much about the angle of the pins or even their exact spacing. The object here is function, not beauty **(photo 4)**.

Cut out the pins. Using a dovetail saw, cut along the lines you've just drawn

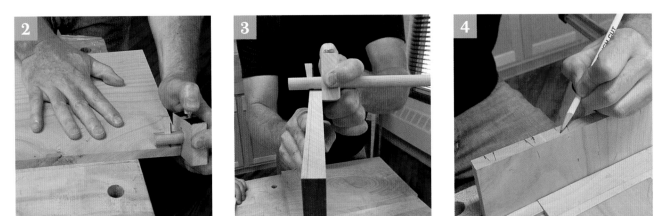

down to the scribe lines. It doesn't matter if you wander a bit over the scribe lines on the bottom edge (**photo 5**). Now, clamp the board to the bench and remove the material between the pins with a chisel (**photo 6**). Repeat the process on the top edge of the side pieces, marking first and then cutting to the scribe lines. Remember, these pins call for precision.

Mark the tails. Transfer the pin locations from the side pieces to the top and bottom pieces (**photo 7**).

T-Mac Tip

If the side pieces are bowed, it will be impossible to transfer the pin locations accurately. If that's the case, clamp a board across the piece to straighten it, then transfer the marks.

Cut out the tails. Transfer the tail lines on the inside faces of the top and bottom across the top with a square. Using a dovetail saw, cut to the lines down to the scribe lines, and remove the material where the pins will fit (**photo 8**).

Test-fit the joints. After cutting out the tails, dry-fit the pieces. If a joint is too tight, pare the inside edges of the tails slightly with a sharp chisel. If you lose patience and try to force the fit, you may end up either splitting or breaking off a few corners (**photo 9**).

T-Mac Tip

If you do break off a piece when assembling the box, save it (if you are lucky enough to find it). You may be able to cover your tracks by gluing it back in place later on.

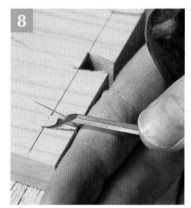

Inspiration from Early American Furniture Makers

Writing desk with tambour doors

My inspiration for the tambour door comes from Federal-style furniture, especially the work of John and Thomas Seymour. This father-and-son team emigrated from England in 1784 and originally settled in Portland, Maine, before they moved to my hometown (Boston, Massachusetts) in 1792.

Some of their work is on display at the Peabody Essex Museum in Salem, Massachusetts, including a writing desk (shown at left), believed to be made by John Seymour. The desk incorporates two tambour doors, a feature the Seymours introduced to American furniture making in the mid-1790s. These doors are made with alternating bands of mahogany and curly maple with a string inlay. The doors slide out to conceal the desk's pigeon holes.

A second Seymour piece at the museum is a sideboard with a beautiful serpentine front that incorporates some elements of British Regency design (see the bottom left photo). This, too, has a tambour door with multiple species of wood.

The slats of these doors are attached to a piece of canvas, allowing the individual pieces to hinge as the doors are opened and closed. That's exactly how the door on our bread box is made.

Tambour door on serpentine front

Sideboard with serpentine front

Making the sides

Make a pattern for the sides. On a piece of ³/₄-in. medium-density fiberboard (MDF) draw a pattern showing the curved outside edge of the side pieces and the groove for the tambour door. The groove should be drawn so that the face of the ⁵/₁₆-in.-thick tambours will be below the curved outside edge of the sides (**photo 1**). Do this by drawing the outside edge of the groove so it's ³/₈ in. from the edge of the side piece (**photo 2**). The groove should be ¹/₈ in. wide. Drawing everything full scale on the pattern ensures that the grooves won't interfere with the rabbet on the back or the dado for the false back.

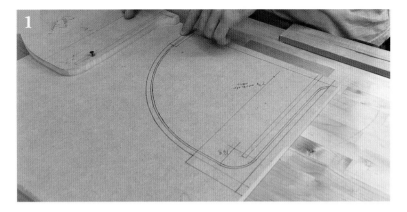

Make a template for the curve. Set up a router with a ¹/₈-in. bit for the groove and a collet to guide the cut (**photo 3**). The offset from the edge of the collet to the bit determines how much smaller the actual template for the sides should be than the pattern. Cut the template to size on the bandsaw and smooth the edges to a fair curve.

Cut the grooves. A reference block screwed to the edge of the template will keep it correctly oriented on the bottom of the workpiece (**photo 4**). Use another gauge block to secure the back of the template to the back edge of the workpiece. When the template is located correctly, screw it to the inside face of each side piece and then clamp the assembly securely to the bench. Now cut a ³/₁₆-in.-deep groove with the router (**photo 5**). Flip the pattern over and cut the groove on the other side piece (**photo 6**).

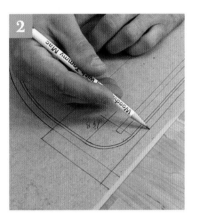

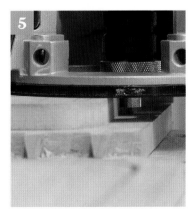

Finishing the box

Cut the rabbet for the back. The two shiplap back boards fit into a $3/8$-in. by $3/8$-in. rabbet cut into the sides, bottom, and top. Set up a stack dado set on the tablesaw and cut the rabbets **(photo 1)**. Set the dado to $1/2$ in. wide, and bury $1/8$ in. of the blade into a sacrificial fence.

Cut a stopped groove for the false back. The tambour door is protected on the inside of the box by a false back set into a groove. The groove must stop before it hits the groove created for the tambour door **(photo 2)**. This is done on a router table by making a stopped cut in one side piece and a plunge cut in the other side piece. Mark the outside faces of the side pieces so you know where to start and stop the cuts. The groove is run all the way through the bottom piece.

Trace and cut the curve. Working from the outermost edge of the groove, set a compass to $1/4$ in. and draw the curves on the side pieces **(photo 3)**. Make sure the curved cut will stop at the edge of the top piece **(photo 4)**. Now cut the sides to shape on the bandsaw.

Fair the curves. Place the two side pieces face to face in a vise with the back and bottom edges perfectly aligned. Using a rasp, file, or electric sander (or another

tool of your choice), fair and smooth the outside curves (**photo 5**). Take your time and work slowly and carefully. Don't go past the layout lines. Then clean up the file marks with 150-grit sandpaper.

Dry-fit the box. Assemble the box (without glue) and take measurements for the front and the false back.

Cut the tenons on the front piece. Cut the $^3/_{16}$-in. by $^3/_{16}$-in. tenons on the ends of the front piece using a dado blade on the tablesaw (**photo 6**). The outside face of the front piece should be flush with the sides of the box, keeping in mind the tenon won't be centered. You'll have to change the blade height after making the first pass over the dado. Creep up on the fit by slowly raising the blade to cut the back face of the tenon.

Glue up the box. Glue and clamp the pieces of the box together (**photo 7**). Clamping pressure is enhanced by using the offcuts (the pieces leftover from cutting out the sides) as cauls. As you'll see, this will allow the sides and the bottom to be pulled tightly together. Don't forget to insert the false back before you glue up the box.

With the box assembled and glued, it's time to make the tambour door (see Making a Tambour Door on pp. 116–119). Once the door is complete you'll be ready for the final steps, which include sanding the completed project with 150- through 220-grit sandpaper, applying a few coats of nontoxic salad bowl finish, and then attaching the back boards.

Making a Tambour Door

To hold the slats in place while they are being glued to the canvas, you'll need to first make a jig from a piece of plywood.

Making the jig

The jig should have two stops, one at either end, and a pair of hold-downs to keep the slats flat. You'll also need two wedges that are used to tighten the slats against each other.

Each of the hold-downs has a rabbet cut in one edge that will lap over the slats **(photo 1).** To calculate the number of slats you'll need, measure the curved opening of the box with a length of string and transfer that dimension to the jig. Draw a line at one end that represents the length of the door. When you have enough slats to reach the mark, the door will be big enough to fit the opening.

Get the length of the slats directly from the box by measuring the distance across the back of the box. Take the measurement from the bottom of the grooves.

Select a board with straight grain, mill it to $7/16$ in. in thickness, and cut it to

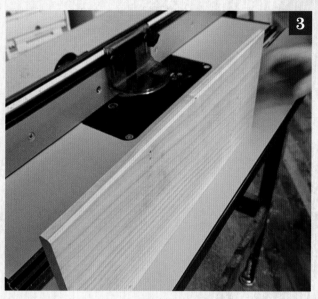

length. Mark the board so the slats can be reassembled in the same order in which they were cut **(photo 2).**

Put the blank in a vise and use a handplane to remove any mill marks on the edge. Take the board to the router table and cut a slight chamfer along each long edge **(photo 3).** Then, slice a $5/16$-in.-thick slat from the blank on the tablesaw. Repeat this three-step process until you have enough slats for the door—it takes about 30 of them.

T-Mac Tip

Using a thin-kerf blade will help get the maximum number of slats out of the blank.

Cut a piece of plywood or MDF longer and wider than the full tambour. Make sure the piece has square corners. Next, attach a stop at each end. The stops should be slightly thinner than the tambour, and they should be parallel to the base. To make the hold-downs, cut them

long enough so they will cover the entire length of the tambour door and extend past the stop. Cut rabbets into the hold-downs. They need to be slightly shallower then the slats and only about $1/4$ in. wide. Screw one hold-down in place, keeping it perpendicular to the stops. Predrill the other hold-down but don't attach it. Next, make two wedges that are about the same thickness as the stops and long enough to span all of the slats. It's a good idea to have on hand extra stock that is the same thickness as the stops and wedges, to use as a spacer if needed.

Assembling the door

Place all of the slats face down, edge to edge, on the jig, maintaining the order in which they were cut. Loosen the hold-down so the slats fit under the rabbet. Next attach a second hold-down so the rabbet covers the other end of the slats **(photo 4)** (p. 118). If necessary, adjust the hold-downs so they stay tight against the ends

of the slats. Then add the wedges and the spacers between the slats and back stop so the slats are squeezed tightly together and sit firmly up against the front stop **(photo 5).**

Now, clamp the jig to the bench and lightly handplane the backs of the slats so they are all completely flush **(photo 6).**

Lay out a piece of canvas and cut it so that it measures 2 in. narrower than the full width of the slats and a couple of inches longer than the full length of slats. The added length will allow you to attach the handle. Once cut, wash and dry the canvas several times before going any further.

With a putty knife or a small paint roller, spread an even coat of glue on the back of the slats, staying 1 in. from the hold-downs. Lay the canvas backer onto the glue and gently smooth it out. Don't press so hard on the canvas that the glue actually penetrates the material. If that

happens, it will make the tambour too rigid to slide smoothly in the grooves. Once the canvas has been applied, allow the glue to dry overnight (don't clamp it down).

Set up a dado set on the tablesaw with a sacrificial fence. Set the fence and the blade so the blade will cut a rabbet that is 3/16 in. wide on the top outside edges of the tambour door, leaving a tenon 1/8 in. thick. Run both sides of the door over the blade to cut the tenons **(photo 7).**

Working from the back of the box, work the door into the grooves. If it gets too tight or starts to bind, back the door out and make whatever adjustments are necessary until the door slides smoothly in its track. You may have to take a bit of material off the tenons with a chisel or plane or even cut the shoulder of the tenons back slightly with a plane to get the door to slide smoothly. When you're done, apply a coat of wax to the tenons.

T-Mac Tip

Don't take too much material off when adjusting the fit of the door. The object is to get the door to slide smoothly, not to make a sloppy fit.

Cut a slat that's double the width of the others, then cut a tenon in each end and work the slat into the grooves of the box. Trap the remaining strip of canvas between the wide slat and a backer piece and screw the two together **(photo 8)**. You'll have to work from inside the box, and that can be tight. Trim away any excess canvas with a knife or chisel. Finally, glue a small piece of wood to the front face of the wide slat for a handle.

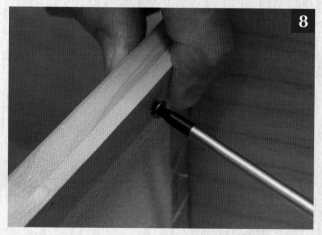

BLANKET CHEST

Mastering Frame-and-Panel Construction with Carved Panels

Blanket chests like this one have been made in Massachusetts since the 1600s. They were originally built in the Pilgrim era, and early examples still can be seen at museums and period homes like the Whipple House in Ipswich, Massachusetts (see my Road Trip on p. 124).

Although it looks complicated, the chest is assembled with basic frame-and-panel construction. It gets its special character from the details: the carved panels on the front of the chest; the beaded profiles and chamfers cut into the legs, rails, and muntins; and the decorative pins where frame members intersect.

Inside, the edges of the panels are raised and a pine bottom has been added.

The lid is kept flat with two battens, which double as hinges. Other than the brass screws that hold the battens to the lid and the screws to the bottom, there's no hardware needed for this project.

Of all the details, the relief carvings on the front panels are the most dramatic, and they are much less challenging than they appear. The carvings can be made entirely with hand tools or with a combination of power and hand tools (see Build Your Skills on pp. 134–135 for more on carving by hand and machine).

This chest is made from quartersawn white oak with a pine bottom. The oak not only has beautiful figure but is also extremely tough and will hold up for generations to come.

Blanket Chest

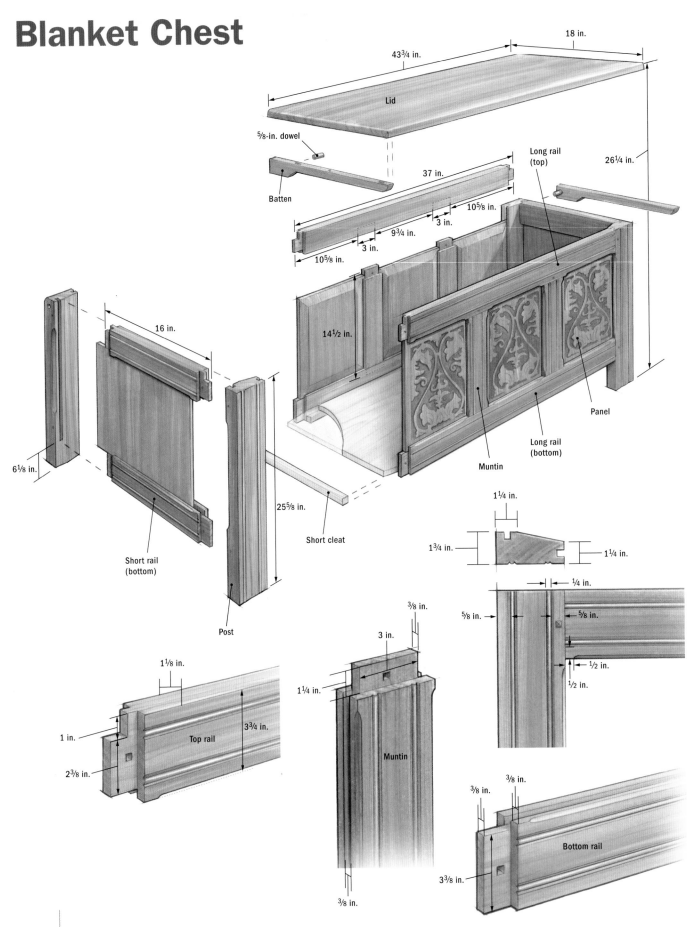

18 in.

43³/₄ in.

Lid

26¹/₄ in.

⁵/₈-in. dowel

Batten

Long rail (top)

37 in.

10⁵/₈ in.

3 in.

9³/₄ in.

3 in.

10⁵/₈ in.

14¹/₂ in.

Panel

16 in.

Long rail (bottom)

Muntin

6¹/₈ in.

1¹/₄ in.

1³/₄ in.

1¹/₄ in.

Short rail (bottom)

25⁵/₈ in.

Short cleat

¹/₄ in.

⁵/₈ in.

⁵/₈ in.

¹/₂ in.

¹/₂ in.

Post

1¹/₈ in.

3 in.

³/₈ in.

1 in.

3³/₄ in.

1¹/₄ in.

Top rail

2³/₈ in.

Muntin

³/₈ in.

³/₈ in.

³/₈ in.

³/₈ in.

Bottom rail

3³/₈ in.

³/₈ in.

MATERIALS LIST/ROUGH MILL

PART	# OF PIECES	LENGTH (IN.)	WIDTH (IN.)	THICKNESS (IN.)	WOOD	NOTES
Posts	4	26⅞	4¼	1⅞	Primary	
Long rails	4	38	4¼	1¼	Primary	
Short rails	4	17	4¼	1¼	Primary	
Muntins	4	15½	4¼	1¼	Primary	
Front and back panels	6	13¾	10¼	⅞	Primary	
Side panels	2	13¾	10¼	⅞	Primary	
Lid	1	44¾	19	⅞	Primary	
Battens	2	18½	2	⅞	Primary	
Long cleats	2	35½	1¼	⅞	Primary	
Short cleats	2	14½	1¼	⅞	Primary	
Bottom	1	40¾	15¼	⅞	Secondary	
Hinge pins	2					1½-in. × ⅝-in. maple or oak
⅝-in. dowels	2	2				
Screws	6					#10 × 1¼-in. brass wood screws

Rough dimensions are slightly longer, wider, and thicker than finished dimensions. Mill the stock, sticker it overnight, and then bring pieces to the finished dimensions the following day.

TOOL LIST

POWER TOOLS
Bandsaw
Drill press
Jointer
Mortising machine
Planer
Router
Router table
Tablesaw with dado blade

HAND TOOLS
Chisels
Clamps
Combination square
Gouges
Hammer
Handplane
Handsaw
Heat gun
Mallet
Marking gauge
Nonmarring dead-blow hammer

Making the frames

The front and back of the chest are frame-and-panel assemblies, each consisting of two posts, a top and bottom rail, two intermediate muntins, and three panels. The chest is completed with rails and a single panel on each end. In laying out the parts for the frame from rough stock, consider grain and color and make your selections so the parts are a good match visually **(photo 1)** (p. 125).

Rough-mill the parts. Each of the pieces should be cut 1 in. longer, ½ in. wider, and ⅛ in. greater in thickness than the finished dimensions (see the Materials

The Long Pedigree of Blanket Chests

Carved semicircular shapes common in 14th-century furniture

Unseasoned lumber that was used to make the chest

The stylistic origins of this project can be traced to a 350-year-old chest at the John Whipple House in Ipswich, Massachusetts. While this beautifully carved chest was made in America using native materials, its decorative style and construction techniques clearly have their roots in England.

On the face of the chest are a number of semicircular shapes carved near the top edge. But if you look at them closely, you will see the patterns could form a series of gothic arches, an element that was common in English churches of the 14th and 15th centuries.

This "dennis chest" was built by a joiner, Thomas Dennis. The trade preceded cabinetmaking, in what's called the First American Period, sometime in the mid-1600s. The European design motifs of this period later spread into American furniture making, which makes this chest a classic example of that influence.

The chest was made from green, unseasoned lumber cut down from lush oak trees harvested from North American forests. The chest includes 28 separate mortise-and-tenon joints and was so solidly built that its condition is as good now as the day it was finished.

List/Rough Mill on p. 123). They should acclimate overnight before being remilled to their final dimensions.

Mark the pieces. To keep everything organized as the parts are machined, mark them with chalk **(photo 2).** Be sure to mark which edges of the frame pieces get grooves for panels **(photo 3);** doing so will minimize the potential for cutting the grooves into the wrong edge.

Cut the grooves. Grooves in the top rails, bottom rails, and muntins are cut the full length of the pieces on the tablesaw using a stacked dado set. To ensure that the grooves of corresponding pieces line up correctly, mark all of the reference faces with an X. When making the grooves on the tablesaw, make sure your reference faces are all facing the same direction and sitting up tight against the rip fence. Adjust the fence so there's a $^3/_8$-in. gap between it and an inside tooth of the dado blade **(photo 4).** Set the blade $^3/_8$ in. high. This will center the groove in the center of the $1^1/_8$-in.-thick rails and muntins **(photo 5).** Now, cut the grooves into the rails and muntins **(photo 6).** Remember rails get only one groove on one edge and muntins get two.

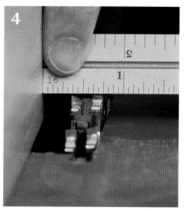

Cutting stopped grooves in the posts

Unlike the grooves in the rails and muntins, the grooves in the legs are stopped at the point where the rails intersect them (**photo 1**). Like the grooves in the rails and muntins, the stopped grooves are also cut on the tablesaw using a stacked dado set but with a slightly different procedure.

Identify stop and plunge cuts. Each post gets a groove on two adjacent edges, but they are cut using different techniques with the tablesaw. One is a stop cut and the other is a plunge cut. It's useful to mark the top of the posts with an "S" or a "P" to differentiate between the two different cuts (**photo 2**).

Mark the fence. On both stop and plunge cuts, you must know where the outside edges of the dado blade sit within the tablesaw insert. With the blade set at a $3/8$-in. height, use the body of a square or a block of wood to mark the outside edges of the blade. Extend these lines up and onto the top edge of the fence, then mark them "S" or "P" (**photo 3**).

Make the stop cuts. To make a stop cut, mark the post where you want the groove to end (**photo 4**) and then run the blank over the blade until that line intersects the "S" line marked on the fence.

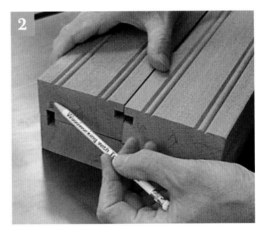

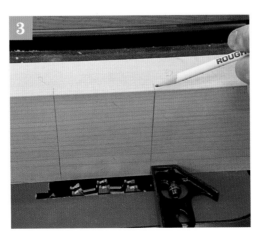

Make the plunge cuts. To make a plunge cut, line up the posts with the "P" mark on the rip fence, then mark the post end closest to you also on the rip fence. **(photos 5 and 6).** Next, securely clamp a solid wooden block on your post-end mark **(photo 7).** This will prevent the post from kicking back as it's lowered onto the blade. When you're ready to make a cut, turn on the saw and lower the blank onto the blade slowly **(photo 8).** Make sure to use a push stick when the post is exiting the blade **(photo 9).**

T-Mac Tip

If making plunge cuts on the tablesaw feels uncomfortable or unsafe, choose another way to make the grooves—with a router or a router plane, for example.

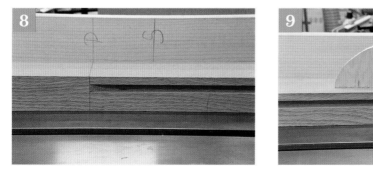

Cutting mortises and tenons

The posts are mortised for the rails on two adjoining edges; the front and back rails are mortised for the muntins. The mortises are really extensions of the grooves—the same width but 1⅛ in. deeper. On the posts, the mortises will clean up the rounded ends of the stopped grooves (**photo 1**).

Lay out the mortises. When you lay out the mortises, don't forget to subtract an amount equal to the depth of the groove. That's because some material on the rails and muntins will be lost when the tenons are cut. If you make the mortise as wide as the rail blank, it will actually be ⅜ in. too long after the tenon is cut (**photo 2**).

Cut the mortises. I cut mortises on a dedicated mortising machine (**photo 3**), but if you don't have one, you can use a router, drill press, or mortising chisel and mallet.

Make the tenons. One way of making tenons on the ends of the rails and the muntins is with a stacked dado set on the tablesaw (**photo 4**). Tenons on the top rails are haunched, meaning a short stub is left to fill the top of the groove (**photo 5**). This makes a stronger joint than a plain tenon would.

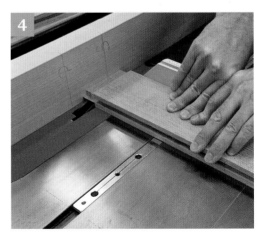

Dry-fit the tenons. After cleaning up the insides of the mortises with a chisel (**photo 6**), dress the faces of each tenon with a shoulder plane (**photo 7**), checking the fit with its corresponding mortise frequently. Dry-fit the frame pieces to make sure everything fits properly. One good thing about working with white oak is you can bang it together without hurting anything. A nonmarring dead-blow hammer really helps with the assembly (**photo 8**).

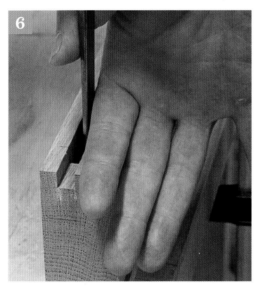

Glossary

Wood movement
is the seasonal
expansion and
contraction of wood
due to changes in
relative humidity.
Wood shrinks when
humidity is low and
expands as humidity
increases.

Adding panels, chamfers, and beading

Size the panels. After dry-fitting the front and back frames, it's time to take measurements for the panels. Start by marking the rails, posts, and muntins $3/8$ in. back from the edge; the lines represent the depth of the groove (**photo 1**). Now measure between the lines to find the width and height for each panel (**photo 2**). Subtract between $1/8$ in. and $3/16$ in. from the width to allow for seasonal wood movement. You're then ready to cut the panels to their final dimensions.

Lay out the chamfer locations. The chamfers along the inside edges of the rails, posts, and muntins dress up what would otherwise be a plain front. They start $1/2$ in. in from where the frame pieces intersect (**photo 3**) and are cut with a chamfering bit on a router table. An easy way to mark the start and stop lines for the chamfers is by using a small block of $1/2$-in.-thick plywood as a guide (**photo 4**).

Set the router table fence. Adjust the split fence on the router table so the width of the opening corresponds to the points where the bit will first encounter wood (**photo 5**). By aligning the layout marks on the backs of the chest

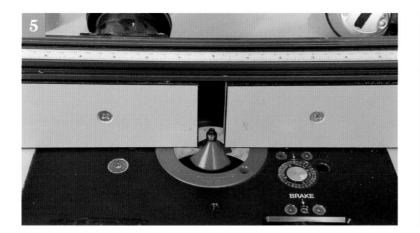

pieces with the edges of the fence, I know exactly where the chamfers will start and stop **(photo 6).** Marking the areas that get chamfers with chalk helps prevent mistakes.

Cut the chamfers. Move the stock over the bit, making sure that it's tight against the fence. When you reach a point where the chamfer should end, pull the stock away from the fence **(photo 7).**

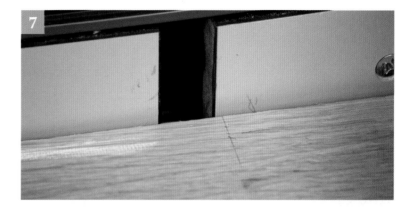

Cut the beading. The beading also is cut on a router table. The beading profile is the same distance in from each edge, which means the bit needs to be set at only one height. To cut the beads, keep the face up against the fence. Run one bead, flip the board end for end, and run your second bead with the same face against the fence.

It's a good idea to set the cut so the center of the bead is slightly ($^1/_{32}$ in.) below the face **(photo 8).** This prevents you from flattening out the bead when you start to clean up the front of the chest with sandpaper.

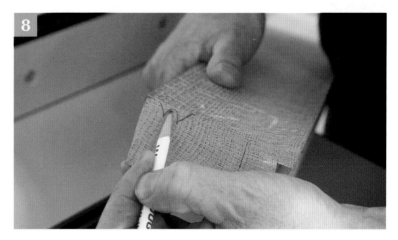

Detailing panels and posts

There are two details I use on the inside of the chest: tapered post corners and raised panel edges. Both contribute to a more finished look.

Taper the inside post corners. The posts would look too blocky if it weren't for a taper along the inside edges of the front and back **(photo 1)**. To set up the cut, make a mark $^3/_{16}$ in. in from where the rails meet the post and connect the marks with a straight line **(photo 2)**. Set the tablesaw blade by eye and make the cuts **(photo 3)**.

Mark the panels. The original Pilgrim chests probably wouldn't have had the raised panel detail inside, but I think it's a nice touch **(photo 4)**. The bevel starts $^3/_8$ in. in from the face of the panel and $^3/_8$ in. back from the edge **(photo 5)**. The taper ends $1^3/_4$ in. from the edge.

Raise the panels. Once the angle is marked on the edge, adjust the tablesaw blade to match it **(photo 6)** and make a couple of test cuts, creeping up to the line.

Once the angle is determined, cut all four sides of the panel **(photo 7).** Remember, just the inside faces of the panels are raised and for now only the panels on the sides and the back of the chest. The taper will be cut on the three front panels after the front faces have been carved (follow the instruction in Relief Carving by Hand and Machine on pp. 134–135).

Relief Carving by Hand and Machine

The carved panels on the chest add character. Back in the Pilgrims' day, the carvings would have been done with a V-tool and gouges **(photo 1),** but today a plunge router can remove most of the waste; a few carving tools do the rest.

The carvings start with a pattern (see the facing page). My first one was paper, but I've since made one from metal, which I use to trace the design directly onto the face of the panel **(photo 2).**

Start by removing the waste with a router. Use a ¼-in. straight bit set to cut about ¹⁄₁₆ in. deep or slightly more **(photo 3).** Working carefully, remove the material in the field between the lines **(photo 4).** To get into smaller areas in the pattern, switch to a smaller bit **(photo 5)** or complete the pattern by hand with carving tools.

The edges of the pattern will be rough at this point, so the next step is to further define the lines with gouges. The pattern has been created using several different gouges, each with a different curve or sweep **(photo 6).** To smooth the lines, simply use the same gouges working your

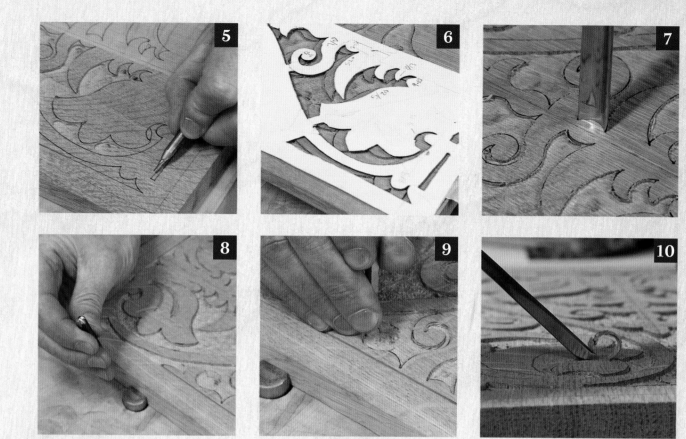

way around, and pick the appropriate tool for a particular area **(photo 7)**. The curves will be an exact match.

The relieved area of the carving is dimpled with a couple of simple tools you can make yourself—a ¼-in. metal pin and a screwdriver tip shaped with a file, or whatever you have around the house. I used a door hinge pin **(photo 8)**. The dimpled surface is created by tapping your tool of choice with a hammer **(photo 9)**. I start with the screwdriver and work around the edges, then use the pin to make a star-shaped pattern on the rest of the surface.

The last of the carving (the patterns in the flowers) is done by hand with a V-tool and mallet **(photo 10)**. When you're done, clean up the face of the panel with 150-grit sandpaper, then cut the bevels on the back of these three panels just as you did on the others on pp. 132–133.

Photocopy carving pattern to approximately 287% to fit panel.

Assembling the chest and adding the top

Glue up the case. Lay out the pieces for the front frame-and-panel section on the bench and glue the muntins into the bottom rail. Then slide the panels into place, beginning with the one at the center, and add the top rail **(photo 1)**. Be careful not to use so much glue that it oozes into the grooves, which would trap a panel. Add the posts and clamp everything together. Repeat the process for the back assembly. Once the glue in these sections has set, glue in the side rails, add the side panels, and clamp the chest together.

Make the hinges. The hinges are wood battens that pivot on short lengths of ⅝-in. dowel. The battens are made from scrap about 1½ in. wide and just a hair shorter than the top is wide. At one end of each batten blank, drill a ⅝-in.-dia. hole with the center located ¾ in. from both the top and the back edge **(photo 2)**. The hole should be about ½ in. deep. Lay out corresponding holes in the upper back corners of the chest with a marking gauge. Place a scrap of veneer beneath the gauge as you strike the marks, which will move the batten slightly up and back for better clearance **(photo 3)**. The holes in the case should be about 1 in. deep **(photo 4)**.

Radius the back edge. In order for the top to open and close without binding, the back edge of the top rail must be rounded over. I use a ⁵/₈-in. roundover bit in a router. Clamp a block on each end of the frame before making the cut to prevent any blowout on the chest posts **(photo 5),** and make the cut in two or three passes. Don't try to remove all the material in a single pass or you'll put too much strain on the router.

Shape the battens. After the holes for the dowels have been drilled, mark out the finished shape of the batten so the arm will be about ⁷/₈ in. thick and cut to the line using a bandsaw **(photo 6).**

Add the top. After the top is glued up and sized to the chest (don't forget to add enough length to cover the battens),

use a ³/₄-in. roundover bit to soften the profile of the front and the two ends **(photo 7).** Leave the back square. Drill three holes through each batten and screw one of the battens to the end of the top. Add the dowel pivots to the chest and place the top on the chest. Then engage the second batten with its dowel and clamp the batten in place. Now you can open the lid and screw the second batten in place **(photo 8).** The top should open and close smoothly. If the top binds, remove a little more material from the back edge using a handplane.

Adding the bottom and finishing up

All that's left is to add the bottom, put in the decorative pins at the mortise-and-tenon joints, and finish the outside of the chest.

Install the cleats for the bottom. The bottom of the chest rests on cleats that are glued in place (**photo 1**). Attach them so the bottom edges are flush with the bottoms of the rails.

Add the bottom. The bottom of this chest is made from white pine, but some people might prefer cedar. Whatever material you chose, leave a small gap all the way around for seasonal movement (**photo 2**). When the bottom has been fitted, run a couple of screws up through the cleats from the bottom to hold it in place.

Insert the pins. Back in the Pilgrim era, the mortise-and-tenon joints would have been held tightly together with draw-bore pins. The pins on our chest are strictly decorative because the joints are already glued together. Start with $3/16$-in. squares of oak scrap, cut them into sections a couple of inches long, and run one end in a pencil sharpener to give it an even taper (**photo 3**). Mark the location of each pin where the muntins meet the rails and where the rails meet the posts, and then drill $3/16$-in. holes about $5/8$ in. deep. Add a dab of glue and tap the pins in with a hammer. I like to set the pins on a diagonal (**photo 4**).

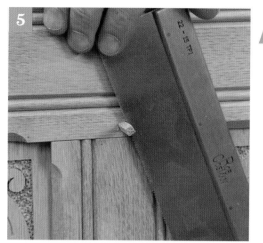

Glossary

A **draw bore** is a type of pinned mortise-and-tenon joint assembled without glue. The hole (or "bore") in the tenon for the pin is slightly offset. As the pin is driven home, it "draws" the pieces together tightly.

Trim the pins. With a fine-tooth saw, trim the pins nearly flush to the surface, taking care not to scratch the surface (**photo 5**). Shape the ends of the pins into a pyramid shape with a chisel, using a prying motion and a piece of scrap to protect the chest (**photo 6**).

Finish the chest. Original chests of the era would have been painted, but I prefer wax because it shows off the natural beauty of the oak. I apply the wax with a soft cloth and buff it out to a soft luster (**photo 7**). I use this same technique inside the chest as well. One or two applications will do the trick.

T-Mac Tip

Wax can catch in all the nooks and crannies of the carvings, making it hard to smooth out evenly. Use a heat gun, set to its lowest setting, to warm the wax and melt it into the wood.

CHIPPENDALE FOOTSTOOL

TECHNIQUE

Carving a Ball-and-Claw Foot

If you've never carved a ball-and-claw foot, this project will have its challenges. For those who've already tried, you may still find it challenging. The process takes practice, but the results are very rewarding.

Will Neptune, a master carver and furniture maker who mentored many woodworkers as a North Bennet Street School teacher, developed the approach that I follow (see my visit with Will in the Road Trip sidebar on p. 144).

It's not obvious how you can coax a round ball clutched by the talons of a bird from square stock. The mystery is solved when you break down the process into a number of simple and straightforward steps. Before launching into the complete project with expensive materials, it's a good idea to practice carving on smaller, less expensive blocks of wood.

Central to the Chippendale style is the cabriole leg, which is laid out with a pattern and cut in two steps on the bandsaw (see Build Your Skills on pp. 146–147).

Despite its elaborate appearance, this project doesn't require an arsenal of carving tools or a lot of material. Everything needed for the legs, rails, and transition pieces came from a single piece of 12/4 mahogany about 6 ft. long and about 8 in. wide.

In addition to the mahogany needed for the footstool, there's also a slip seat made out of ash, along with webbing, horsehair, cotton batting, and decorative fabric. It's best to consult with an upholsterer for this part of the project.

Even if you don't want to tackle this entire project, learning how to carve a ball-and-claw foot is well worth your time.

Chippendale Footstool

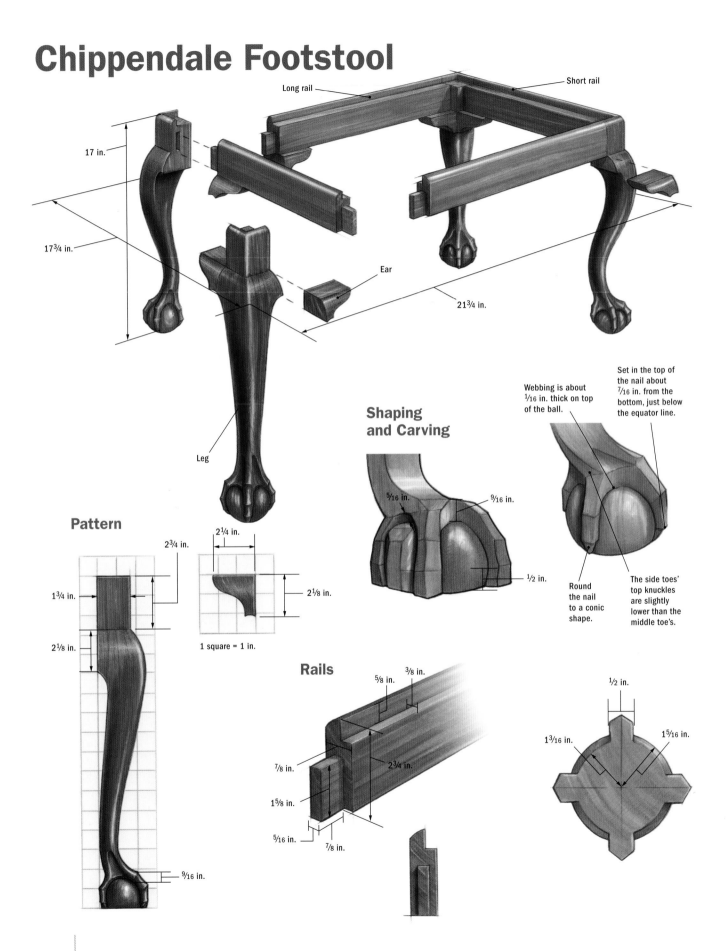

Long rail

Short rail

17 in.

17³⁄₄ in.

Ear

21³⁄₄ in.

Leg

Shaping and Carving

Webbing is about ¹⁄₁₆ in. thick on top of the ball.

Set in the top of the nail about ⁷⁄₁₆ in. from the bottom, just below the equator line.

⁵⁄₁₆ in.

⁹⁄₁₆ in.

¹⁄₂ in.

Round the nail to a conic shape.

The side toes' top knuckles are slightly lower than the middle toe's.

Pattern

2³⁄₄ in.

2¹⁄₄ in.

1³⁄₄ in.

2¹⁄₈ in.

2¹⁄₈ in.

2¹⁄₈ in.

1 square = 1 in.

⁹⁄₁₆ in.

Rails

⁵⁄₈ in.

³⁄₈ in.

2³⁄₄ in.

⁷⁄₈ in.

1⁵⁄₈ in.

⁵⁄₁₆ in.

⁷⁄₈ in.

¹⁄₂ in.

1³⁄₁₆ in.

1⁵⁄₁₆ in.

MATERIALS LIST/ROUGH MILL

PART	# OF PIECES	LENGTH (IN.)	WIDTH (IN.)	THICKNESS (IN.)	WOOD
Legs (includes transition pieces)	4	23	2⅞	2¾	Primary
Long rails	2	19¼	3	1	Primary
Short rails	2	15¼	3	1	Primary
¼-in. plywood for pattern	23	2⅞			

Rough dimensions are slightly longer, wider and thicker than finished dimensions. Mill the stock, sticker it overnight, and then bring pieces to the finished dimensions the following day.

TOOL LIST

POWER TOOLS
Bandsaw
Circular saw
Jointer
Mortising machine
Planer
Tablesaw with dado blade

HAND TOOLS
Chisels
Clamps
File
Gouges
Handplane
Handsaw
Mallet
Marking gauge
Rasp

Laying out the legs

Mill the stock. From a plank of 12/4 mahogany, mill four leg blanks and four rails. Leave enough length in the leg stock to allow for two transition blocks, or ears, per leg. If possible, mill the legs so the grain goes diagonally across the top, which is called rift-sawn (**photo 1**).

Cut the ears off. Next, cut off the ears from the leg blanks and mark them so they can be oriented correctly later (**photo 2**).

Trace the pattern. In addition to providing a template for the curves of the leg pattern, it also provides details that will help develop the ball-and-claw foot (**photo 3**) (p. 145). Trace the paper pattern onto a piece of ¼-in. plywood, which will be more rigid and survive multiple tracings. Working with your pattern, you'll then trace the outlines of the legs, making sure the back of the pattern is flush with the inside corner of the leg. The tracings will end up being mirror images of each other (**photo 4**) (p. 145).

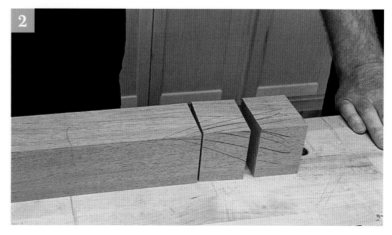

Visiting the Master of the Carved Foot

Will Neptune in his shop

New York foot

The Boston foot

The method for making ball-and-claw feet that's taught at North Bennet Street School was developed by Will Neptune, a master carver and furniture maker (see the top photo at left).

The ball-and-claw foot actually originated in China as a tiny pearl being held in the claws of a dragon. It evolved into a form with a much larger ball and eventually came to the American colonies from England. By the mid-18th century, the style had become very popular.

There are several variations. The classic New York foot, shown in the center photo at left, is a little flatter and more static looking, you could even say clunkier, than some of the others. The Boston foot (shown in the bottom photo at left) has heavily raked talons, with the toe curled dynamically around the ball, making it much harder to carve. The Philadelphia foot, which Neptune used

to demonstrate his technique and the same one I'm creating for this stool, has a nice curvature in the side toes and a graceful sweep to the ankle. The toes flow smoothly from the ankle, as shown in the bottom left photo.

The challenge of the ball-and-claw foot is visualizing a round ball emerging from the square stock and then applying a systematic approach to creating it. Neptune, who has been developing this system for the past 30 years, starts by laying out the bottom of the ball on the stock and then he gets to work (see the photo below).

Coaxing a round ball from square stock

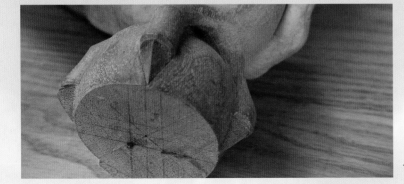

The Philadelphia foot

Cut the mortises. Lay out the mortise locations. Then, with the back of the blank against the fence of the mortising machine, cut the mortises. These $5/16$-in. mortises are set back from what will be the front of the leg post by $5/16$ in. and are stopped $1\frac{1}{8}$ in. short of the end of the leg so a rabbet can be cut for the seat (**photo 5**).

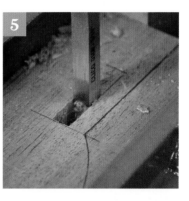

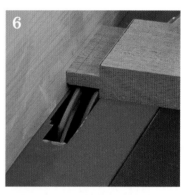

T-Mac Tip

Clamp a stop block to the fence of the mortiser to locate the leg blanks correctly. This also allows you to set your stops on the mortising machine.

Make the tenons. With a stacked dado set on the tablesaw, cut tenons in the ends of all the rail pieces (**photo 6**). These tenons are $7/8$ in. long. Cut the two cheeks first and then, without moving the fence, adjust the blade height and cut the shoulder on the tenon.

Cut the rabbets. Using a stacked dado set on the tablesaw, cut a rabbet $3/8$ in. deep and $5/8$ in. wide on the inside edges of the rails (**photo 7**).

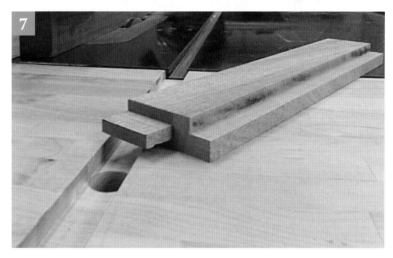

Cutting Out a Cabriole Leg

Although carving the ball-and-claw foot is the technical highlight of this project, the graceful curves of a cabriole leg are central to the Chippendale style. After the pattern has been traced on the blank, the leg is ready for the bandsaw **(photo 1)**.

It's crucial to stay outside the lines, particularly at the ankle where the leg meets the foot **(photo 2)** and at the top of the leg where the square post meets the curve that forms the knee. It might be useful to sketch a second line outside the pattern line to provide a small safety margin.

With the traced pattern facing up, cut to the lines **(photo 3)**.

You'll need to restore the lines that have been cut away in order to cut the other side. Simply tape the offcuts back

on the blank with masking tape; this will also make the blank less tippy **(photo 4).** Retrace the pattern on the blank where the lines are obscured by the tape.

Rotate the blank 90 degrees and cut to the layout lines **(photo 5).** The blank is now ready for shaping and carving **(photo 6).**

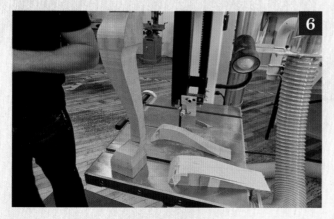

Shaping the legs

Place the leg in a vise. Mount a bar clamp to a length of wood, place the wood in a vise, and then clamp the leg in the bar clamp (**photo 1**). To avoid shearing off part of the leg, don't exert too much pressure with the clamp and keep the pressure centered over the ankle of the leg, not the outside of the foot.

Fair the curves. With a spokeshave or a rasp, fair the curves on the leg (**photo 2**). The surface doesn't have to be perfect, but the curves should be smooth. Work toward the ankle and make sure to leave the layout lines at the ankle.

Lay out the chamfer. Beginning at the midpoint of the angle, sketch lines up the leg to mark the point where the square stock will become rounded (**photo 3**). The leg will be completely rounded at the ankle transitioning to larger, flatter areas near the top. Next draw a second set of lines outside of the first ones indicating where you'll start the chamfer (**photo 4**).

Cut to the line. With a very sharp chisel or a rasp, cut away the sharp corners of the leg, working to the first set of layout lines. Then work the corners to the second layout line to bring the leg to a well-rounded shape.

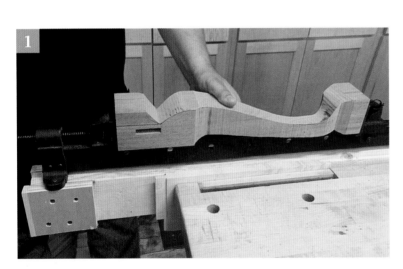

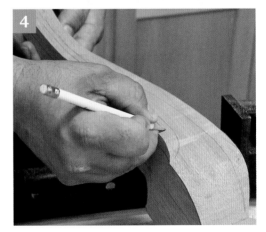

Carving the feet

It's now time to start on the main event, carving the feet. If you've never tried this before, don't dive into your expensive mahogany right away. Work on some practice blocks in a wood like poplar, basswood, or some scrap around the shop. With time, you'll get the hang of it—without the added stress of working with expensive wood. You can get two practice feet out of a 12-in.-long piece of stock 3 in. sq. Working from both ends, lay out each foot using the first 6 in. of your pattern.

Lay out the bottom of the foot. Find the center of the leg on the bottom of the blank and with a compass draw the largest circle that will fit inside the stock. Then make a second circle slightly inside the first to represent where the ball will curve inward and meet the floor (**photo 1**). At each corner, mark the location of the toes, and continue those lines up the outside of the blank to indicate the width of the toes (**photo 2**).

Draw the equator line. To help shape the bottom of the foot, draw a pencil line ½ in. up from the bottom to represent the widest part of the ball, or equator, on the foot (**photo 3**).

Cut to the lines. Clamp the leg in the vise and using a dovetail saw or any kind of handsaw, cut along the toe layout lines toward the outermost circle, the equator of the ball (**photo 4**).

Form the ball. With a sharp chisel, pare to the equator line to form a circle at the bottom of the leg (**photo 5**). If you go too far with the chisel and take off part of the toe, just remember that's the purpose of working on practice blocks.

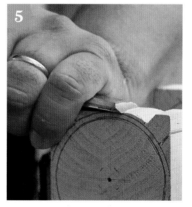
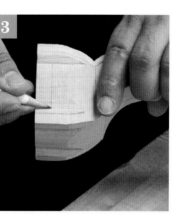
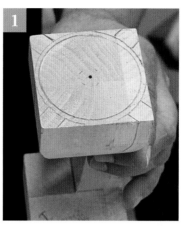
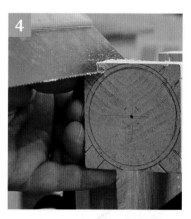
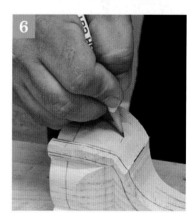

Find the top of the ball on the outside faces. Starting at the ridge left by roughing out on the bandsaw, mark a point ⁹⁄₁₆ in. down on the two outward faces of the leg (**photo 6**). Now, with a 5/20 gouge, make a series of cuts to begin forming the top of the ball, working from the ridge toward the mark you've

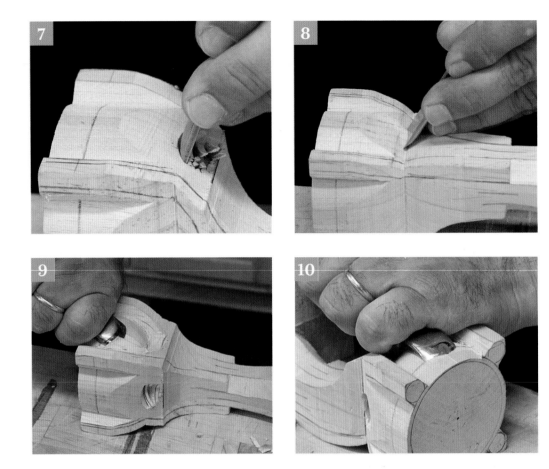

just made (**photo 7**). Make the cuts with the gouge straight up, perpendicular to the axis of the leg. It takes practice to learn how deep to make these cuts, but remember that you are trying to get a ball out of this piece of stock. Visualize the shape and let that be your guide.

T-Mac Tip

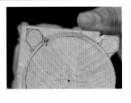

Be conservative. Remember, you can't put wood back after you've carved it off, so go slowly and don't work past your layout lines, as I did here.

Form the back of the ball. On the back two faces of the leg, the cut defining the top of the ball is different, as indicated by the pattern. Here, the gouge goes in at a 45-degree angle, not straight down (**photo 8**), and is only about 5/16 in. deep.

Shape the ball. Using the same gouge, work from the equator line toward the top of the ball on both sides of the back toe. As you do this, follow the imaginary horizon of a sphere (**photo 9**). Make rolling stab cuts along the edges of the talons to help define the edges of the ball. Use firm pressure on the gouge, and be careful not to remove too much material from either the ball or the talons. Now work the bottom of the ball, starting from the equator down (**photo 10**).

Making the toes

Lay out the chamfer. Sketch in the cross section of each toe on the bottom of the leg, and then draw lines extending up both sides of the toe blank to mark the start of the chamfer (**photo 1**). At the ankle, these lines will meet and blend into the chamfer lines you previously made on the upper portion of the leg (**photo 2**).

Pare the corners. Secure the leg in the clamp and, with a sharp chisel, pare to these layout lines (**photo 3**). Then use a veiner to scoop out the material between the toes (**photo 4**).

Carve the knuckles. Mark out the knuckles, the first slightly above the equator line, then use a chisel and a backbend gouge to give the knuckles shape and definition (**photo 5**). Keep an eye on the grain of the wood as you work, and reverse directions with the tool when you start to encounter tearout.

Carve the nails. Shape the nail at the end of the toe with a chisel (**photo 6**). You can then start cleaning up the leg—but not too much. Remember, this is a hand-carved leg and you don't want to eliminate all of the tool marks that give your piece its individual character.

After practice blocks, carve the real thing. It will take some time, but once you've got a good idea of how the foot takes shape it's time to put away the practice blocks and carve the bottom of each leg. Don't expect perfection right away.

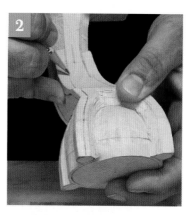

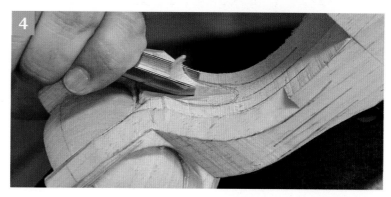

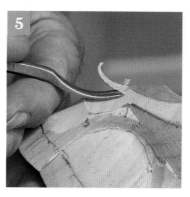

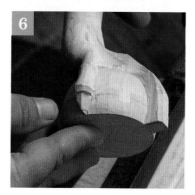

Finishing the legs

Trim the leg posts to shape.
Assemble the legs and rails and mark the outside of the post where the rail intersects it (**photo 1**). Then take the frame apart and cut off the excess on each leg at the bandsaw (**photo 2**).

Glue the frame together. After all of the legs have been trimmed, it's time to assemble and glue all eight pieces together.

Make the transition pieces.
Orient the blocks saved from cutting the legs so the grain matches the legs. Mark out the transition curve from the leg pattern as well as the curve of the leg (**photo 3**). Cut out the transition pieces on the bandsaw and glue them to the frame of the stool in their correct positions.

Do the final shaping. Using chisels and a shoulder plane, carefully smooth the area where the transition blocks, legs, and rails meet (**photo 4**). Now remove the material at the top inside of the leg so the leg profile matches the rabbets you've already cut on the rails. You can do this using a router or with a chisel and mallet. You may also want to round over the top outside edges of the rails into a softer profile.

Making the slip seat

Making a slip seat involves some time and probably some materials you don't normally keep around the shop. One option is to have the seat made by a local upholsterer, but if you want to try it yourself, here's what you have to do.

Make the frame. Using ³/₄-in.-thick by 2½-in.-wide hardwood, make a frame to fit inside the rabbeted recess in the top of the stool. The corners of the frame are connected with slip joints. (For more on making slip joints, see Making the Top Frame on p. 39.)

Fit the frame into the recess and mark along the edge where the edge of the frame should be beveled to meet the rails and legs **(photo 1).** You can cut the bevels on a tablesaw.

Attach the webbing. Weave pieces of upholstery webbing to cover the top of the frame, attaching the pieces with upholstery tacks. Cover the webbing with a piece of burlap, wrapping the edges to the back of the frame, and tack that down.

Add horsehair padding. Place a mound of horsehair on top of the burlap and arrange it into a gently domed shape **(photo 2).** The horsehair should be 6 in. or so thick at the center and tapered out toward the edges. Follow that with a layer of muslin, which will hold the horsehair in place, and then by a layer of cotton batting. The horsehair, muslin, and cotton batting will be held in place by decorator fabric, which will be stretched tightly over the top. You'll want to fold the edges beneath the frame, and tack them in place **(photo 3).** The seat is held in place by the rabbeted recess and doesn't need any fasteners.

Add the finish. When the slip seat is complete, the stool is ready for your finish of choice. Pop the seat out so you don't get any finish on the fabric and apply the finish. I used a coat of linseed oil followed by shellac and then a dark wax that adds a century of patina instantly.

TRELLIS

TECHNIQUE

Cutting and Fitting Dadoes

A trellis is a quick project that doesn't have any complicated joinery (or even glue) and uses readily available materials. It will also make a sweet addition in the garden or on the side of your house.

This trellis is constructed of two posts, four crossmembers, and nine vertical slats, all held together with dado joinery and stainless-steel screws. Choosing sturdy materials and fasteners appropriate to outdoor conditions is the key to durability. Making a trellis that can't handle the weather, or the vegetation growing on it, means a short life span (see my Road Trip to Peacefields, the Adams Homestead, in Quincy, Massachusetts on p. 158).

The central decorative element of this trellis is the diamond-shaped pattern at the center and the corresponding half-diamond shape at the top. While it's not entirely necessary, this decorative element adds a lot to the finished design, and it's easy to create.

The heartwood of redwood, cypress, and cedar is resistant to both decay and insects. Any of them would be a good choice for this project. I chose red cedar for this project, and any it didn't need any finish.

Trellis

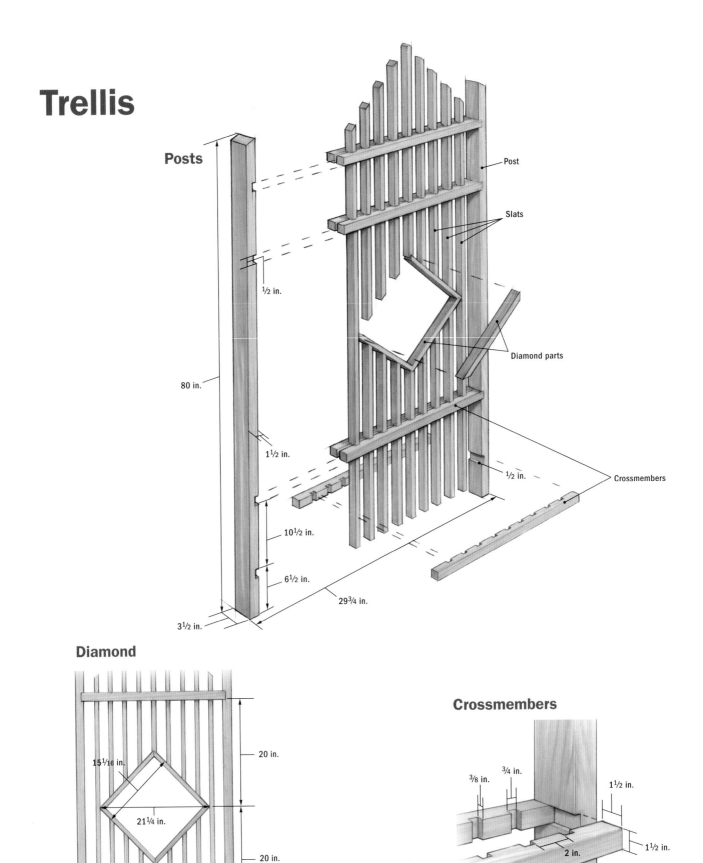

Posts

Post

Slats

½ in.

80 in.

1½ in.

Diamond parts

½ in.

Crossmembers

10½ in.

6½ in.

29¾ in.

3½ in.

Diamond

20 in.

15¹⁄₁₆ in.

21¼ in.

20 in.

Crossmembers

⅜ in.

¾ in.

1½ in.

2 in.

1½ in.

MATERIALS LIST/ROUGH MILL

PART	# OF PIECES	LENGTH (IN.)	WIDTH (IN.)	THICKNESS (IN.)	WOOD	NOTES
Posts	2	81	4	1¾	Primary	
Crossmembers	4	28¾	4	1¾	Primary	
Vertical slats	9	76¾	¾	1¼	Primary	
Diamond parts	4	16⅙	¾	1¼	Primary	
Stainless-steel screws	16					#8 or #10 × 2 in.
Stainless-steel trim head screws	30					#8 × 2 in.

Rough dimensions are slightly longer, wider and thicker than finished dimensions. Mill the stock, sticker it overnight, and then bring pieces to the finished dimensions the following day.

TOOL LIST

POWER TOOLS
Bandsaw
Drill
Jigsaw
Miter saw
Planer
Tablesaw with dado blade

HAND TOOLS
Handsaw

Cutting posts and crossmembers

Cut the posts. After squaring up one end of each 2×4 post, cut the tops to a 15-degree angle (**photo 1**). Make sure the posts are exactly the same length.

Cut the dadoes. The inside of each post gets four dadoes, ½ in. deep and 1½ in. wide, which are cut on the tablesaw with a ¾-in. stack dado set. The edge of the first dado is 6 in. from the end of the post. You'll make the dadoes in two passes. First, clamp a piece of ¾-in. material to the fence. On the first pass, register the end of the post against this block; on the second pass, register the end of the post to the fence itself (**photo 2**). This will produce a dado 1½ in. wide. Flip the post end for end and repeat, then move the fence over 12 in. and cut the other two dadoes.

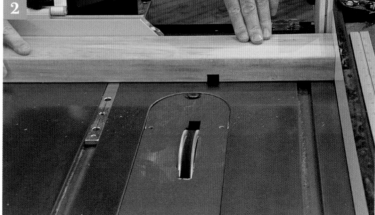

A Lesson in Choosing Materials

A trellis is a framework of wood or metal that supports flowers or vines. It can be a freestanding structure or attached to the side of a building, where it adds architectural definition just as porch columns do.

That's the case with the trellises at Peacefields, the Adams's homestead in Quincy, Massachusetts, home of two U.S. presidents. Visiting the Adams's house is a good reminder to choose weather-resistant materials and fasteners and to scale a trellis appropriately for the plant it will support. One large trellis along the front of the Adams's house supports a massive grapevine; it was painted to protect the wood from decay, a finish that was appropriate to the decor of its time.

Another trellis attached to an original brick house hasn't been as lucky. This aging trellis is more than two stories high and has become overburdened by a massive wisteria vine. It was constructed from exterior-grade wood—which is now in poor condition.

The Adams's House

Make the crossmembers.
There are four crossmembers $27^3/_4$ in.
long, each with a series of $^3/_4$-in. dadoes
cut on the inside face for the slats. The
crossmembers are made by cutting the
dadoes in each 2×4 (**photo 3**), then
ripping the 2×4s in half on the tablesaw.

T-Mac Tip

To ensure all the crossmembers are the
same length, invest the time in setting up
a stop block on your miter saw rather than
measuring and marking each member
individually.

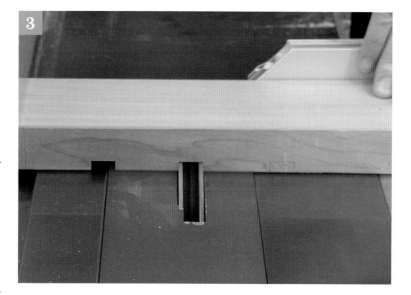

Mill the crossmembers to fit.
After ripping the crossmembers in half,
run them through the thickness planer
on edge until they fit snugly in the dadoes
in the posts (**photo 4**). Mark the ends of
each pair of crossmembers as they come
off the saw so they can be matched up
correctly at assembly.

**Attach the crossmembers on
one side.** Lay the posts out on the
bench and fit the crossmembers for one
side of the trellis into the dadoes. Then
drill a pilot hole through the side of each
post into the end of each crossmember
and drive in a stainless-steel screw
(**photo 5**). Make sure the outside of the
crossmember is flush with the outside
edge of the post.

Adding the slats

Make the slats. There are nine slats, each ³/₄ in. by 1¹/₄ in., cut from 2×4s. Before ripping the slats, set the tablesaw fence to 3³/₈ in. and remove the chamfered edge of the 2×4 **(photo 1).** Then put the freshly cut edge of the 2×4 against the fence, set the width of the cut for ³/₄ in., and cut out the slats **(photo 2).** You should be able to get three slats from each 2×4. Cut the slats to a width of 1¹/₄ in.

Cut the slats to 45 degrees. Eight of the slats are cut at 45 degrees at the top. Six of them are cut at about the midway point at 45 degrees to form the diamond pattern at the center of the trellis. On a miter saw, cut the top of one slat. Set the stop on the saw to make a second cut about midway down the slat. Slide the slat down to the stop and make a second cut at 45 degrees **(photo 3).** Repeat with the other five slats. The outermost slat on each side should remain at full length, with only the top cut at an angle.

Make the center slat. The remaining slat will be the center slat. Cut the top to form a peak with two 45-degree cuts meeting at the center. At the midway point, where the slat will meet the diamond, lay out two 45-degree lines that meet at the center and remove the V-shaped waste with a handsaw or bandsaw **(photo 4).**

Flip the bottom pieces. Set the slats into their dadoes, then roll the lower parts of the slats 180 degrees so the 45-degree miters face the other way **(photo 5).**

Install the other crossmembers.
Fit the four remaining crossmembers into their corresponding dadoes in the post and screw them in place through the sides of the post as done previously.

Lay out the diamond. Measure the distance between the inside faces of the two outermost slats and divide that by two. Mark the two outer slats at the halfway point and place a straightedge across the slats, then measure up from the straightedge the same distance. This is where the bird's mouth of the center slats should be located **(photo 6).** Tack the center slats in place by drilling through the crossmember and driving in a trim-head screw.

Make the center square. The diamond at the center of the trellis is really just a square set on a diagonal. To find the dimensions of the pieces, measure from the midway mark on the outer slat to the center of the bird's mouth **(photo 7).** Cut four pieces of slat material with a 45-degree miter on each end to this dimension.

Complete the pattern. Tack the outer slats in place, slide the other slats out of the way temporarily, and fit the four pieces that make up the diamond between the outer slats and the bird's mouths in the center slats. When you slide the slats down to meet the sides of the diamond, you will have created the corresponding diamond shape on the top and bottom of the trellis.

Now, pin all of the slats in place by drilling pilot holes and screwing them down through the two center crossmembers. Screw the diamond pattern pieces in place into the ends of the slats **(photo 8),** and trim the bottom slats to length with a jigsaw.

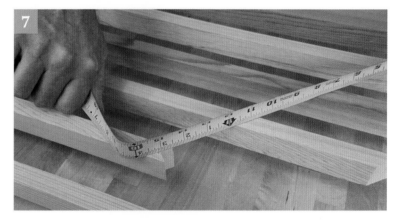

FINISHING

TECHNIQUE

Working with Oil, Shellac, and Wax

Finishing furniture is an art. You can create a beautiful piece of furniture but prep it incorrectly or apply the wrong finish, and it will never reach its full potential. My favorite finish is a combination of oil, shellac, and wax, which protects the surface, illuminates the depth, and enhances the figure and color of the wood. From time to time I also like to use lacquer, tung oil, and varnishes.

The walnut trestle table on pp. 18–31 is used to illustrate the basic steps of surface preparation and finishing. The key to any good finish is how you prep furniture for a finish—you need to get rid of mill marks, tearout, glue residue, sanding marks, and any other surface defects.

I like to use a combination of power tools, hand tools, and abrasives to repair these problems. Train yourself to inspect surfaces carefully. Some problems may not look serious when the wood is raw, but they become much more pronounced after the finish has been applied. Finishing takes patience; go step by step and take your time.

Shellac is one of my favorite finishes because of its clarity and the depth of color it coaxes from wood. It's a natural product and is available in spray form or premixed in a can, but I like using the dry flakes that get mixed with denatured alcohol. For some tips on choosing and mixing shellac, I visited with a master finisher (learn more from my visit in the Road Trip sidebar on pp. 174–175).

TOOLS

POWER TOOLS

Random orbit
  sander

HAND TOOLS

No. 4 or
  no. 4½
  bench
  plane
Card scraper
Sandpaper
Mill file
Sharpening
  stone
Burnisher
Clean,
  lint-free
  rags

Dealing with mill marks and tearout

Some surface problems are best addressed before a piece of furniture is assembled. That's the time when surfaces are accessible and individual components are easy to move around. Two of the most common problems that are always present when using power tools are milling marks (horizontal lines that are left by a jointer or planer) **(photo 1)**, and tearout (broken fibers that occur when a tool exits a cut).

Removing mill marks. The best way to remove mill marks is with a no. 4 or no. 4½ handplane. Make sure the plane is razor sharp. Work your way methodically across the width of the board, and you'll start to see the mill marks disappear **(photo 2)**. Don't go too deep—the idea is to clean up just the surface **(photo 3)**.

T-Mac Tip

You can apply a little paraffin wax or any wax over the bottom of a handplane to make the tool glide smoothly over the surface of a piece of wood.

Handplane tearout carefully. The best way to deal with tearout is with a no. 4½ high-angle handplane and a card scraper. On a no. 4½, the blade is set at a higher-than-usual angle, allowing the wood fibers to be cut at a more abrupt

angle **(photo 4).** Adjust the blade so it's taking off very little material. Watch the shaving as it comes off the blade and adjust the blade so the shaving is of a uniform thickness. If you keep getting tearout in one area, try turning the board around so you're planing from the opposite direction **(photo 5).**

Switch to a card scraper. You may not be able to get rid of all the tearout with a plane, especially in figured wood. Some areas may be too difficult to fix.

That's when it's time to reach for a card scraper **(photo 6),** an indispensable tool in my shop. A card scraper is just a piece of sheet metal with a tiny burr along the edge. Scrapers come in a variety of shapes and sizes. The one I'm using here is a standard rectangular-shape scraper. To use it properly, place your thumbs on the back side, flex it slightly, and push the scraper across the surface **(photo 7).** You may have to experiment to find the angle that cuts most effectively. You should get

continued on p. 168

Glossary

A **burr** is a minute hook along the edge of a scraper that allows you to shave the surface of a piece of wood gently. It's produced with a tool called a burnisher.

Sharpening a Card Scraper

A card scraper can make quick work of smoothing a surface. Sharpening is not difficult, but it does take a bit of trial and error. Clamp the scraper firmly in a vise **(photo 1)** and with a mill file go over the edge lightly until the old burr is gone. You will feel the straight edges of the scraper with your fingers when the burr has been removed **(photo 2).**

Although you could use the burnisher to create a burr now, it's better to hone the sides of the scraper first. You'll get a better, longer-lasting burr. Remove the scraper from the vise and hone each side on a stone (a 1,000-grit stone works well) **(photo 3).** You'll know you're finished when you feel a clean, square edge on the tool with the tip of your finger.

Safety First

Be careful when sharpening a scraper. It's easy to slip and gouge your wrist or hand on the corners of the scraper.

At this point you're ready to form a burr on the edge. Put the scraper back in the vise and make sure it's well clamped. This is when you need to be especially careful not to slip off the edge of the scraper with your burnisher. Work slowly and apply light pressure.

To create a burr, I prefer using a triangular burnisher **(photo 4).** Go back and forth a few times over the edge of the scraper **(photo 5).** This action will start to warm up the metal and make it easier to form the burr. Don't apply too much pressure. Once you feel the edge of the scraper starting to change shape, it's time to adjust the angle of the burnisher slightly to complete finishing the burr **(photo 6).**

Once you've created the burr, the scraper is ready to be used. The key to using it effectively is to locate the angle you created with the burnisher. With scraper in hand, make test passes over your board until you find your cutting edge. You'll know you've found it when you get a clean, well-formed shaving and not dust **(photo 7).**

T-Mac Tip

Use honing oil or any oil when creating the burr on the scraper. It allows the burnisher to glide easily over the metal.

beautiful, paper-thin shavings (**photo 8**) as you smooth the surface (**photo 9**).

Scrapers are very effective tools, as long as you know how to sharpen them. For more, see Sharpening a Card Scraper on pp. 166–167.

When using a card scraper, remember "easy does it." Overdoing it with a sharp scraper can create a deep divot in the surface of the wood that you will then have to go back and flatten out (**photo 10**). Another note of caution: When you're trying to remove an area of tearout, don't overwork it. It's best to work the area around the tearout as well, feathering out the repair until each area is smooth.

T-Mac Tip

A card scraper can get hot enough to burn your thumbs. Put a refrigerator magnet on the back of the card to insulate your fingers. You can also try putting a rubber sewing thimble on each thumb to provide protection.

Working with a random-orbit sander

A random-orbit sander is a great tool for cleaning up irregular surfaces, but if it's used improperly, it can leave ring and swirl marks that are really obvious once the finish has been applied (**photo 1**).

Keep off the edges. Grinding the surface with the edge of the sander is one cause of swirl marks (**photo 2**). The best way to avoid creating these marks is by keeping the sander flat and going over the entire surface lightly. Never approach the surface of the wood with the edge of your sander (**photos 3 and 4**).

Use the right grit. Choose the right paper for what you're trying to accomplish. An 80- or 100-grit paper can remove a lot of material quickly, but when it comes to getting a smooth finish, you'll need to switch to 180- or 220-grit paper, possibly even finer.

Finish with a sanding block. After you've finished with the orbital sander, wrap a piece of 150- or 220-grit sandpaper around a sanding block and go over the surface again, moving in the direction of the grain (**photo 5**). Look at the surface carefully, and if you see any remaining orbital sanding marks, just keep working the surface until they are gone.

Dealing with glue squeeze-out

Glue residue usually shows up as a white or yellow discoloration around a joint (**photo 1**). Glue left on the surface seals the wood so finish can't penetrate, making the problem very obvious when the finish is applied.

Use a wood block or your fingers. Glue may show up where two pieces of wood come together at right angles, making it difficult to hand-sand the area without creating cross-grain marks. In this situation, use a block of wood to protect one piece of wood while sanding up to it (**photo 2**). Alternately, use your fingers to prevent the sandpaper from wandering over the line and creating cross-grain scratches (**photo 3**). There's no chance you'll mar the wood with a block this way, and if there are any cross-grain marks they'll be on a very small scale. After sanding in one direction, work up to the line from the other side, repeating the process (**photo 4**).

Sand out cross-grain marks. Cross-grain sanding scratches can be handled the same way as glue residue. Protect the grain direction on one piece

of wood (with a wood block or your fingers) while sanding by hand the cross-grain marks on the other piece of wood. Remember to always sand with the direction of the grain **(photo 5).**

Break the edges. Finishes can bead up and roll off the sharp edges of a tabletop. To prevent that from happening, break the sharp edge slightly to create a softer profile. You can use sandpaper **(photo 6)** or, for a more pronounced roll, hit the edge with a card scraper before applying the finish.

T-Mac Tip

Spend whatever time you need to remove all traces of glue from the parts of your project that will be seen. Don't worry about hidden recesses that can't be seen. Pick and choose your battles.

Removing dents

Dents in the surface of the wood are usually caused by dropping something on the surface (**photo 1**). The temptation may be to sand just the area where the dents appear, but that's going to create a noticeable divot. So the trick is to tackle a broader area and feather out the repair over a wider area surrounding the dent (**photo 2**).

A good tool for this job is an in-line sander, also called a half-sheet sander because its pad is big enough for a half-sheet of sandpaper. It covers a broad area and makes it a little less likely that you'll create a divot (**photo 3**).

T-Mac Tip

If you're using a sander with dust collection, drape the hose and power cord over one shoulder as you work. Doing this will keep both cords out of the way and prevent them from scraping along the edge of the workpiece.

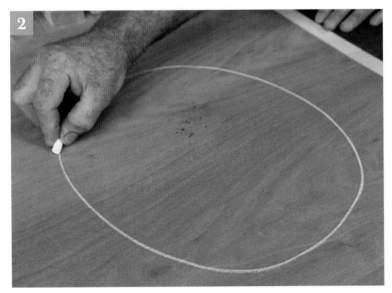

Cover a broad area. Work the entire area around the dents **(photo 4)**. Eventually, even the deepest dents will be gone. Be patient and keep going until the surface is completely uniform **(photo 5)**.

Hand-sanding is an alternative. If you don't have a pad sander, you can use a block of wood and various grits of sandpaper to attack the dented area **(photo 6)**. Start with 100-grit paper and work your way progressively through 150-grit sandpaper until the dents are gone **(photo 7)** and the surface is smooth. Whether you sand by hand or with a power sander, the most important thing is not to stay in one area but to feather out the repair.

Hit the entire surface. Once the glue and dents are gone, go over the entire surface with a pad sander or sanding block. Use 150-grit paper to remove all discoloration and get the top to a uniform smoothness **(photo 8)**.

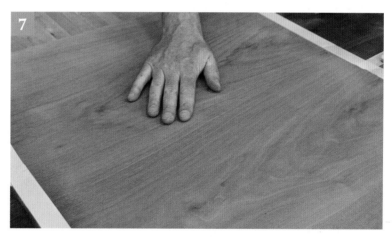

Shellac: An Old Finish That Still Excels

Lumberyards and hardware stores stock dozens of clear finishes for wood. Whether they are water or oil based, many of them are complex chemical formulations that are far different from the finishes used by earlier generations of furniture makers.

Shellac is an exception. It's a natural product derived from the secretions of the lac bug, an insect that lives in the forests of India and Thailand, and it's been used as a furniture finish for centuries.

To get a better historical perspective on how finishes have evolved and to learn more about different varieties of shellac, I visited master finisher Christine Thomson, who is also a specialist in period work.

Furniture of the 17th and early 18th centuries was typically finished with wax and oils. To make a wax finish, beeswax was mixed with turpentine to create a paste. The paste was then scrubbed into the pores of the wood using the edge of a tightly rolled bundle of cloth (photos below).

In the late 18th century, finishers began using film-forming materials. A variety of plant resin varnishes were created by mixing the sap-like resins with water, alcohol, or oils. They all had different properties, and some of them were difficult, even dangerous, to prepare.

Beeswax and turpentine

A cotton applicator

Shellac is a fairly simple (and safe) finish. It dries very quickly and can be applied by brush, pad, or spray gun. Shellac comes in many colors, from very dark to super blond. In its raw form, shellac flakes are very dark, but shellac can be made lighter by refining it further and removing residual wax.

Shellac flakes are dissolved in denatured alcohol to make the finish; 1 lb. of shellac flakes dissolved in 1 gal. of alcohol is called a 1-lb. cut. This is a good general cut that's workable. However, depending on the heat and humidity of the room you are working in, you may need to adjust the viscosity, making it thinner or thicker. Dissolving more flakes in the same amount of alcohol will give you a heavier-bodied finish.

When using shellac, I prefer super blond because of its clarity. The challenge in applying it is that it tends to be a little more brittle and finicky to work with than other varieties.

Shellac is also available in pre-mixed cans and spray cans. While it is much more convenient to use, it does have a shelf life, so be sure to check the expiration date on the label.

Plant resin varnishes

Shellac flakes

Flakes dissolved in alcohol

Applying linseed oil

I agonize over grain patterns, tones, and textures while I'm building a piece of furniture. I like to accentuate all of my hard work with linseed oil and then follow it up with shellac and, finally, wax. Oil brings out the figure and color of the wood, shellac protects the surface and gives it a visual depth, and the wax gives it a warm glow.

Clean the surface. Before applying any oil, wipe down the surface with a lint-free cloth. That's all you need to remove any dust.

Make your oil applicator. Use a piece of clean, lint-free cotton and fold it into a pad (**photo 1**). A big rag will soak up too much oil. It's best to start with a piece of cloth roughly 6 in. sq. that's then folded into a smaller pad. Wet the rag, but don't make it dripping wet (**photo 2**). You're going to be applying a thin sealer coat so it doesn't have to go on too thick.

Start with a circular motion. Begin by applying the oil to the surface in a circular motion (**photo 3**). You should feel the rag pull a little on the surface of the wood, which tells you the rag isn't too dry.

Follow with long strokes. Once you've gone over the surface in a tight circular pattern, follow it up with long strokes going with the direction of the grain (**photo 4**). This helps work the oil deeply into the pores of the wood.

Allow to dry. The oil should dry in about 24 hours, but in humid weather it might take a couple of days before it's completely dry. Be patient.

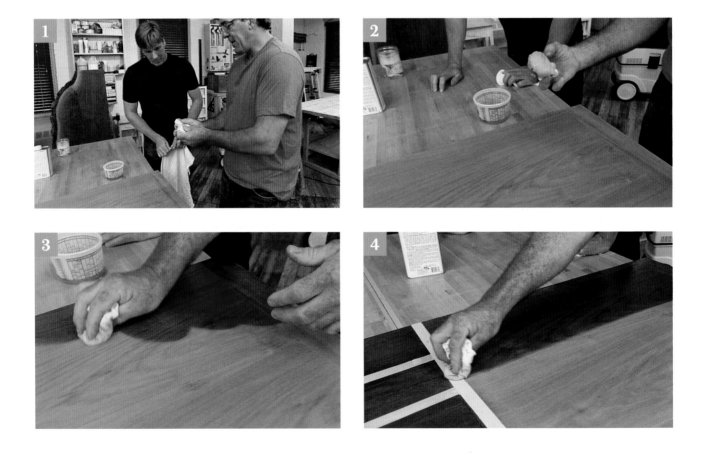

Applying shellac

One advantage of mixing your own shellac is that you know it will dry properly because it's fresh. Premixed shellac that's been sitting around for a year or more may not dry completely.

If you're making your own, start with a 1-lb. cut. If you don't need a full gallon, make a smaller amount mixed to the same proportions.

Here are some tips for applying shellac:

- **Brush application.** One way of applying shellac is with a brush, but speed is essential because the alcohol evaporates very quickly. Always work with the grain and keep a wet edge. **(photo 1).**

- **Don't worry about perfection.** The surface doesn't have to be perfect; if you discover a blemish after the shellac has dried, you can always sand it out later and reapply some shellac—or just live with it.

- **Finish the bottom of the top.** The underside of a tabletop needs to be finished just like the top to help prevent imbalances in moisture content. What you don't have to worry about are minor problems or imperfections because the underside won't be seen.

- **Apply thin coats.** If you're applying shellac with an aerosol can, keep in mind a thick coat won't save you any time. It's just the opposite: You're more likely to create finish defects, including blobs, drips, and buildup of an uneven coat **(photo 2).** Rule of thumb: Thin coats are better.

- **Let the finish dry completely.** It will take several coats to complete the finish. Be sure to allow each coat to dry thoroughly before applying the next. Sand the surface between coats with 320-grit paper, and limit yourself to one coat a day. The number of coats applied to a project is a matter of personal preference. Some like an open-pore finish, which requires fewer coats, and some like a full finish, which requires more. I tend to use three to five coats at a minimum.

Safety First

If you use an aerosol can or spray gun to apply shellac, make sure you wear a respirator and have plenty of ventilation in the room. This can be accomplished with box fans or overhead fans or by opening doors and windows—anything to increase air circulation.

Solving finish problems

There are three common problems with a shellac finish, regardless of whether the shellac is applied with a brush, a pad, or a spray gun: blush, over application of finish, and a finish that won't harden because the oil beneath the shellac hasn't completely cured.

- **Blush.** Blush, which appears as a white haze on the surface, is more likely when the finish is sprayed on. The haze is actually trapped moisture, and it typically occurs in humid weather **(photo 1).** It may look as if your finish were ruined, but it sometimes cures itself if given additional drying time. If the haze hasn't disappeared by the following day, sand the surface lightly and reapply the shellac.

T-Mac Tip

There are times when the best thing you can do is walk away from your project, as is the case with blush. Time alone may sort out the problem—or at least give you an opportunity to see it with a fresh pair of eyes.

- **Over application.** It's not uncommon to apply too much finish in a single coat, especially when you're anxious for the project to be done **(photo 2).** A heavy coat creates finish defects though, so in the end all you're doing is just making more work for yourself. If you apply too much finish, you'll need to aggressively sand down the surface to eliminate blobs, drips, and buildup, and then reapply a thin coat of finish.

- **Oil that hasn't dried.** If the linseed oil hasn't cured thoroughly before the shellac is applied, then the shellac itself won't dry **(photo 3).** You'll know this has happened when the finish appears to be bumpy and when you start to sand your project the paper clogs quickly with small flecks of oil and shellac **(photo 4).** To fix this problem you'll need to lightly sand down the surface with 320-grit paper until the paper no longer clogs and the result from sanding is a fine thin powder.

As oil accumulates on your sandpaper, flip it over to expose a fresh face then keep sanding.

After fixing any surface problems, build up the surface with new applications of shellac. Apply light coats and sand in between with 320-grit paper, building up the finish until you're satisfied with it. Don't forget to allow adequate drying time between coats. When to stop is a matter of personal preference, but after applying the last coat, you may notice that the surface has a rough, almost pebbly texture and a high sheen **(photo 5)**. The solution is to sand one last time, but use a light hand so you don't sand through the finish to bare wood.

T-Mac Tip

Instead of using a commercial grain filler, dip your shellac pad into shellac, followed by oil, and then pumice. Work the mixture into the pores. Start with a circular motion, and then finish up with straight strokes that move in the direction of the grain.

Finishing up

The finish may seem complete, but for some added protection for your shellac surface, consider applying a thin coat of wax. Here's what to do.

Sand the surface one last time. After the final coat of shellac has been applied, sand the entire surface once again lightly with 320-grit paper to remove any bumps or ridges in the finish (**photo 1**). Don't sand too heavily, and be careful not to rub through the shellac to bare wood. Sand with the grain and use light, even pressure. As the sandpaper gets clogged with powder from the finish, fold it to expose a new face. Inspect the surface periodically to make sure you're removing all of the minor surface imperfections that remain (**photo 2**).

Choose your wax. There are many different kinds of wax. You'll have to experiment to find the one you like. On the walnut trestle table I am using a dark-colored wax that will complement the color of the wood—it won't change the color of the wood, just enhance it.

Prepare the pad. Start with a small square of lint-free rag, roughly 6 in. sq., and fold it up into a small pad. It's best if you can put it in the can of wax and leave it for a day or two before using it. The rag will soak up liquids from the wax (**photo 3**) and do a much better job than if you have to scoop wax out of the can with a dry rag. When you're ready to apply the wax, remove the rag from the can and just blot the surface of the wax lightly to pick up a little more wax.

Rub it in. Apply a thin coat of wax to the surface, working first in a circular pattern and then shifting to long strokes that move in the direction of the grain (**photo 4**).

Let it dry. After the wax has dried for 10 or 15 minutes, buff it out with a clean rag (**photo 5**). When buffing, long strokes are best because the even pressure will create a uniform, protective coat with a warm luster and sheen.

Inspect and resand if needed. After the wax has been buffed out, you may see imperfections remaining on the surface. If that's the case, sand them out lightly with 320-grit sandpaper. At this point, you can sand lightly across the grain without creating a problem. Applying the wax isn't a one-shot process. You may think you're done, but you'll keep discovering surface flaws that need to be addressed. Finishing is a work in progress. Be patient because the results will be worth it (**photo 6**).

T-Mac Tip

Don't worry if the final results are not perfect. You may see a ding or scratch that didn't get corrected or a spot where you oversanded. This is not the end of the world. What is important is that you gave your all and created something with your own hands. When making furniture, your project should reflect the best of where your skill level is at the time.

METRIC EQUIVALENTS

Inches	Centimeters	Millimeters	Inches	Centimeters	Millimeters
1/8	0.3	3	13	33.0	330
1/4	0.6	6	14	35.6	356
3/8	1.0	10	15	38.1	381
1/2	1.3	13	16	40.6	406
5/8	1.6	16	17	43.2	432
3/4	1.9	19	18	45.7	457
7/8	2.2	22	19	48.3	483
1	2.5	25	20	50.8	508
1 1/4	3.2	32	21	53.3	533
1 1/2	3.8	38	22	55.9	559
1 3/4	4.4	44	23	58.4	584
2	5.1	51	24	61.0	610
2 1/2	6.4	64	25	63.5	635
3	7.6	76	26	66.0	660
3 1/2	8.9	89	27	68.6	686
4	10.2	102	28	71.1	711
4 1/2	11.4	114	29	73.7	737
5	12.7	127	30	76.2	762
6	15.2	152	31	78.7	787
7	17.8	178	32	81.3	813
8	20.3	203	33	83.8	838
9	22.9	229	34	86.4	864
10	25.4	254	35	88.9	889
11	27.9	279	36	91.4	914
12	30.5	305			

INDEX